OPPOSING VIEWPOINTS® SERIES

North and South Korea

Other Books of Related Interest:

At Issue Series
Does the World Hate the United States?
Is Foreign Aid Necessary?

Global Viewpoints Series
Human Rights

Opposing Viewpoints Series
Dictatorships
Free Trade
Human Rights

"Congress shall make no law . . . abridging the freedom of speech, or of the press."

First Amendment to the US Constitution

The basic foundation of our democracy is the First Amendment guarantee of freedom of expression. The Opposing Viewpoints series is dedicated to the concept of this basic freedom and the idea that it is more important to practice it than to enshrine it.

North and South Korea

Noah Berlatsky, Book Editor

GREENHAVEN PRESS
A part of Gale, Cengage Learning

Detroit • New York • San Francisco • New Haven, Conn • Waterville, Maine • London

Elizabeth Des Chenes, *Director, Content Strategy*
Cynthia Sanner, *Publisher*
Douglas Dentino, *Manager, New Product*

For more information, contact:
Greenhaven Press
27500 Drake Rd.
Farmington Hills, MI 48331-3535
Or you can visit our Internet site at gale.cengage.com

Articles in Greenhaven Press anthologies are often edited for length to meet page require- ments. In addition, original titles of these works are changed to clearly present the main thesis and to explicitly indicate the author's opinion. Every effort is made to ensure that Greenhaven Press accurately reflects the original intent of the authors. Every effort has been made to trace the owners of copyrighted material.

© Giordano Aita/Alamy

LIBRARY OF CONGRESS CATALOGING-IN-PUBLICATION DATA

North and South Korea / Noah Berlatsky, book editor.
    pages cm. -- (Opposing viewpoints)
    Includes bibliographical references and index.
    ISBN 978-0-7377-6963-0 (hardcover) -- ISBN 978-0-7377-6964-7 (pbk.)
    1. Korean reunification question (1945-)--Juvenile literature. 2. Korea (South)--Foreign relations. 3. Korea (North)--Foreign relations. I. Berlatsky, Noah.
    DS917.444.N65 2013
    951.904--dc23
                                        2013002491

Printed in the United States of America
1 2 3 4 5   17 16 15 14 13

Contents

Why Consider Opposing Viewpoints?   11

Introduction   14

Chapter 1: What Are the Issues in the Relationship Between the Koreas?

Chapter Preface   18

1. Reassessing the Sunshine Policy   20
   Moon Chung-in, as told to Evan Ramstad

2. South Korea Should Not Return   28
   to the Sunshine Policy
   John Hemmings

3. Korea Reunification Would Spell Trouble   33
   for Seoul
   Foster Klug

4. Dear Leader's Big Moment for Détente?   39
   Isabel Hilton

5. Lost, Without a Trace   43
   Hideko Takayama and Evan Thomas

6. South Korea's Response to North Korean   49
   Abductions Is Politicized and Inadequate
   Brad Williams and Erik Mobrand

Periodical and Internet Sources Bibliography   62

Chapter 2: What Is the Relationship Between the Koreas and the World?

Chapter Preface   64

1. China's North Korea Policy Is Illogical   66
   and Damages Chinese Interests
   Ralph A. Cossa and Brad Glosserman

2. North Korea: China Weighs Up Opposing North   72
Korea Policies
Anny Boc

3. The United States Should Remove   77
Its Troops from Korea
Doug Bandow

4. The United States Will Not Remove   82
Its Troops from Korea
George Friedman

Periodical and Internet Sources Bibliography   91

Chapter 3: Does North Korea Present a Serious Threat to the World?

Chapter Preface   93

1. A Leadership Transition May Reduce the North   95
Korean Threat
Peter Hayes, Scott Bruce, and David von Hippel

2. The Leadership Transition Shows Little Sign   103
of Reducing the North Korean Threat
Justin McCurry

3. North Korea Is a Serious Nuclear Threat   107
to Australia and the World
Kevin Rudd

4. North Korea Is Not a Serious Nuclear Threat   112
to the United States
Fred Kaplan

5. Talks with the United States Could Reduce   119
the North Korean Nuclear Threat
Evans J.R. Revere

6. Talks with North Korea Would Worsen   129
the Nuclear Threat
John R. Bolton

7. European Participation in Talks Could   134
Reduce the North Korean Nuclear Threat
Philip Worré and Intaek Han

Periodical and Internet Sources Bibliography   138

Chapter 4: What Are Human Rights Issues in North and South Korea?

Chapter Preface   140

1. South Korea Has Exposed Human Rights   142
Abuses in North Korean Prison Camps
Chico Harlan

2. South Korea's National Security Law   148
Violates Human Rights
Kay Seok

3. South Koreans Are Reluctant to Highlight   153
North Korean Human Rights Violations
Iris Chung

4. Portraying North Korea as the Villain   166
on Human Rights Is Unhelpful
Paul Watson

5. North Korea Orchestrates Famine   170
as a Tool of Repression
Robert Park

6. There Are Political Barriers to Providing   181
Food Aid to North Korea
Donald Kirk

Periodical and Internet Sources Bibliography   187

For Further Discussion   188

Organizations to Contact   190

Bibliography of Books   194

Index   197

Why Consider
Opposing Viewpoints?

> *"The only way in which a human being can make some approach to knowing the whole of a subject is by hearing what can be said about it by persons of every variety of opinion and studying all modes in which it can be looked at by every character of mind. No wise man ever acquired his wisdom in any mode but this."*
>
> *John Stuart Mill*

In our media-intensive culture it is not difficult to find differing opinions. Thousands of newspapers and magazines and dozens of radio and television talk shows resound with differing points of view. The difficulty lies in deciding which opinion to agree with and which "experts" seem the most credible. The more inundated we become with differing opinions and claims, the more essential it is to hone critical reading and thinking skills to evaluate these ideas. Opposing Viewpoints books address this problem directly by presenting stimulating debates that can be used to enhance and teach these skills. The varied opinions contained in each book examine many different aspects of a single issue. While examining these conveniently edited opposing views, readers can develop critical thinking skills such as the ability to compare and contrast authors' credibility, facts, argumentation styles, use of persuasive techniques, and other stylistic tools. In short, the Opposing Viewpoints Series is an ideal way to attain the higher-level thinking and reading skills so essential in a culture of diverse and contradictory opinions.

In addition to providing a tool for critical thinking, Opposing Viewpoints books challenge readers to question their own strongly held opinions and assumptions. Most people form their opinions on the basis of upbringing, peer pressure, and personal, cultural, or professional bias. By reading carefully balanced opposing views, readers must directly confront new ideas as well as the opinions of those with whom they disagree. This is not to argue simplistically that everyone who reads opposing views will—or should—change his or her opinion. Instead, the series enhances readers' understanding of their own views by encouraging confrontation with opposing ideas. Careful examination of others' views can lead to the readers' understanding of the logical inconsistencies in their own opinions, perspective on why they hold an opinion, and the consideration of the possibility that their opinion requires further evaluation.

Evaluating Other Opinions

To ensure that this type of examination occurs, Opposing Viewpoints books present all types of opinions. Prominent spokespeople on different sides of each issue as well as well-known professionals from many disciplines challenge the reader. An additional goal of the series is to provide a forum for other, less known, or even unpopular viewpoints. The opinion of an ordinary person who has had to make the decision to cut off life support from a terminally ill relative, for example, may be just as valuable and provide just as much insight as a medical ethicist's professional opinion. The editors have two additional purposes in including these less known views. One, the editors encourage readers to respect others' opinions—even when not enhanced by professional credibility. It is only by reading or listening to and objectively evaluating others' ideas that one can determine whether they are worthy of consideration. Two, the inclusion of such viewpoints encourages the important critical thinking skill of objectively evaluating an author's credentials and bias. This evaluation will illuminate an author's reasons for taking a particular stance on an issue and will aid in readers' evaluation of the author's ideas.

It is our hope that these books will give readers a deeper understanding of the issues debated and an appreciation of the complexity of even seemingly simple issues when good and honest people disagree. This awareness is particularly important in a democratic society such as ours in which people enter into public debate to determine the common good. Those with whom one disagrees should not be regarded as enemies but rather as people whose views deserve careful examination and may shed light on one's own.

Thomas Jefferson once said that "difference of opinion leads to inquiry, and inquiry to truth." Jefferson, a broadly educated man, argued that "if a nation expects to be ignorant and free . . . it expects what never was and never will be." As individuals and as a nation, it is imperative that we consider the opinions of others and examine them with skill and discernment. The Opposing Viewpoints series is intended to help readers achieve this goal.

David L. Bender and Bruno Leone,
Founders

Introduction

"North Koreans call Americans 'Yang Ko Bak Ee' to make fun of their appearances. They have long noses. . . . We were taught that 'Yang Ko Bak Ee should be killed.'"

—a North Korean defector quoted by Jimin Lee in "North Korean Defectors Speak Out," CBS News, December 9, 2010

The United States has a long history of involvement in the Korean Peninsula. When Communist North Korea invaded the south in 1950, the United States sent troops and played a central role in the four-year Korean War. Since the end of that conflict, the United States has maintained a troop presence in South Korea. It has also taken the lead in trying to push North Korea to give up its nuclear weapons program.

Given the US presence in the region, it is no surprise that people in both Koreas have strong feelings about the United States. In fact, anti-Americanism is a powerful force in both North and South Korea.

In North Korea, anti-Americanism is a central ideology of the ruling Communist regime. For example, in 2009, shortly after the United Nations imposed sanctions on North Korea for a nuclear test, the government held a massive ceremony commemorating the outbreak of the Korean War. This ceremony included orchestrated anti-American rhetoric, including one speaker who declared, "Our revolutionary armed forces will deal an annihilating blow that is unpredictable and unavoidable, to any 'sanction' or provocations by the US," according to Choe Sang-Hun in a June 25, 2009, *New York Times* article.

The 2009 rally was a special event, but North Korean anti-Americanism is not merely for special occasions. On the contrary, it is routine and institutionalized. A June 23, 2012, article in *USA Today* quotes an elementary school teacher declaring, "Our children learn from an early age about the American bastards." According to the article, North Korean classrooms are plastered with anti-American posters, and one of the most popular activities at recess is to beat a dummy American soldier with sticks. Children are taught that Americans were responsible for beginning the Korean War and are told that North Korea will eventually exact revenge. In a February 18, 2010, article for *Newsweek*, Isaac Stone Fish quotes the common North Korean maxim: "Just as a jackal cannot become a lamb, the U.S. imperialists cannot change their rapacious nature."

North Korea is a longtime enemy of the United States. South Korea is an ally—but even so, it has its own tradition of anti-Americanism. In a December 2002 survey, for example, 44 percent of South Koreans held unfavorable views of the United States. There are numerous reasons for this high level of antipathy toward Americans. First, the United States is often associated by South Koreans with the authoritarian government that came into power after the war, according to Meredith Woo-Cumings in a July 2003 working paper at the Japan Policy Research Institute. America's close relationship with the dictatorship of Chun Doo Hwan did long-term damage to the United States' image. Other policy decisions—for example, Bill Clinton's ratcheting up of tensions on the peninsula during the 1990s—also alienated many South Koreans, according to Woo-Cumings.

Jimmy H. Koo in a 2011 brief titled "The Uncomfortable SOFA," referring to the status of forces agreement, also points to actions by US troops in Korea as a spur for anti-Americanism. A 2002 incident in which US soldiers en route to a training exercise struck and killed two Korean schoolgirls was particularly inflammatory. It sparked protests and demands that the soldiers be turned over to South Korean jurisdiction. Instead, the soldiers were tried in a US military court, which controversially acquitted them of negligent homicide.

Despite such tensions, however, the relationship between the United States and South Korea remains close—and has in fact grown closer in recent years. In his first term, US president Barack Obama visited Seoul more than any other foreign capital, according to a May 31, 2012, article in the *Economist*. Obama and South Korean president Lee Myung-Bak developed a close working relationship and together crafted the first free trade agreement between the United States and an East Asian nation.

This book looks at controversies involving North Korea and South Korea in chapters titled What Are the Issues in the Relationship Between the Koreas?, What Is the Relationship Between the Koreas and the World?, Does North Korea Present a Serious Threat to the World?, and What Are Human Rights Issues in North and South Korea? In each chapter, different authors present varying viewpoints on the issues that—like anti-Americanism—unite and divide North Korea and South Korea.

OPPOSING
VIEWPOINTS®
SERIES

CHAPTER 1

What Are the Issues in the Relationship Between the Koreas?

Chapter Preface

The Korean Demilitarized Zone, or DMZ, is a 250 kilometer (160 mile) long, 4 kilometer (2 mile) wide strip of land that separates North and South Korea. It is the most heavily militarized border in the world. It is also, surprisingly, a unique wilderness preserve.

The Korean Peninsula, including North and South Korea, is heavily populated. It has also experienced intense military conflict, especially during the Japanese invasion of World War II and the Korean War of the 1950s. Following the wars, Korea rapidly industrialized. As a result of all of these factors, the peninsula has a "severely degraded natural environment" and massive air, water, and soil pollution, according to Lisa Brady in an April 13, 2012, article for the *Guardian*.

While the rest of the peninsula suffered ecologically, however, the DMZ was spared. Created at the end of the Korean War as a neutral buffer zone between North and South Korea, the DMZ is strewn with land mines and closely guarded by troops from both Koreas. For humans, stepping into the DMZ can be deadly.

However, for that very reason, the strip has exploded with wildlife. More than one thousand species of plants and hundreds of species of mushrooms, fungi, and lichen thrive in the area. Rare cranes, fish, amphibians, reptiles, and even mammals have been sighted, including the Asian black bear, the musk deer, and the spotted seal. Scientists believe there may even be tigers living in the DMZ, though the big cats had been thought to have vanished from Korea more than sixty years ago.

While the DMZ has proven a haven, that haven is not secure. If war were to break out between North and South Korea, the DMZ habitat could be destroyed. Alternately, peace between the Koreas could make the DMZ safe for human development—resulting in the widespread destruction of wildlife. Already, some parts of the DMZ have been cleared for agriculture, destroying plants and threatening the ecosystem. Hall Healy, president of the DMZ Forum in the United States that works to protect the DMZ, noted, "As resilient as these habitats have proven to be, they can't sustain this level of development on a broader scale," as quoted by Tim Wall in a February 7, 2012, article for Discovery News.

In response to the danger, activists have begun to work to try to ensure the future of wildlife in the DMZ. As Lee Hong Koo, a former prime minister of South Korea, has said, "I don't find anywhere else like [the DMZ] in the world. We want to preserve it," as quoted by Fiona Harvey in a September 6, 2012, article in the *Guardian*. South Korea has opened some parts of the DMZ to hiking, in the hopes that ecotourism will help to popularize the DMZ as an ecological refuge. Activists are also trying to get legislation passed to officially protect the strip; whether these efforts will be successful is uncertain.

Whatever its ultimate fate, the DMZ is a symbol of how North and South Korea remain simultaneously divided by politics and united by history, ecology, and tradition. The remainder of this chapter examines some of the other important issues in the relationship between these two countries.

> "There is a method of improving human rights in North Korea. There is a priority too. For example, for me, peace is more important than human rights."

Reassessing the Sunshine Policy

Moon Chung-in, as told to Evan Ramstad

Moon Chung-in is a political scientist at Yonsei University and a former advisor to South Korean presidents Kim Dae-jung and Roh Moo-hyun. Evan Ramstad is the Korean correspondent for the Wall Street Journal. *In the following viewpoint, Moon argues that the Sunshine Policy—in which South Korea offered North Korea economic and other aid—was never fully implemented. He argues that opening North Korea to markets will help North Koreans more than confronting the regime about human rights. He argues that the Sunshine Policy would bring increased prosperity and peace, which would benefit both North Korea and South Korea.*

As you read, consider the following questions:

1. Why does Moon argue that the Sunshine Policy was in action for less than a year?

2. According to Moon, why does North Korea care so much about the United States?

3. Why does Moon say that North Korea will accept the Sunshine Policy even though it knows it is intended to overturn the regime?

Should South Korea return to the Sunshine Policy for dealing with North Korea? Moon Chung-in says yes.

Mr. Moon, a Yonsei University political scientist, magazine editor and close advisor to former presidents Kim Dae-jung and Roh Moo-hyun, is so eager to restore the battered reputation of the Sunshine Policy that he's written an English-language book about it.

Mr. Moon hopes to influence the political debate ahead of South Korea's presidential election in December.

Under the Sunshine Policy, initiated by Mr. Kim and continued by Mr. Roh, South Korea reached out to the North with economic aid and passive language in hopes of starting projects that would create a wedge between the North Korean regime and its people, creating the "sunshine" that would lead to greater reforms.

On Sunday, the candidate who is most likely to revive the Sunshine Policy (or major aspects of it) Mr. Roh's former chief of staff Moon Jae-in formally announced he will run for president. Moon Jae-in is a political newbie, having just won his first election, a Busan district seat in the April race for the National Assembly.

In the book, called *The Sunshine Policy: In Defense of Engagement as a Path to Peace in Korea*, Moon Chung-in argues the policy never really got a chance to work.

While most people view the policy as lasting for the ten-year period of the Kim and Roh presidencies, Mr. Moon says that it was in action for less than a year. The reasons: North Korea resisted it for much of Mr. Kim's presidency and the election of George W. Bush as U.S. president in 2000 thwarted its effectiveness until the final months of Mr. Roh's presidency.

Here are extended excerpts from a conversation with Mr. Moon about the book, the political scene and the contradiction of progressives who fought for human rights and democracy in South Korea but won't criticize North Korea's dictatorial regime.

WSJ: *What is the main thing you're trying to get across in the book?*

Mr. Moon: What I wanted to convey to Western readers is very simple. A lot of people say the Sunshine Policy failed. But the longevity of the Sunshine Policy was just nine months. June to December 2000 and October to December 2007. The rise of Bush destroyed everything. And then the Lee Myung-bak government came and derailed everything achieved in the Roh Moo-hyun government. Therefore, it is not ten years of Sunshine Policy. It was less than one year.

You blame the U.S. quite a lot in the book. Why does North Korea care so much about the U.S.?

Memory. During the Korean War, American Air Force strikes destroyed Pyongyang and North Korea. The U.S. is really powerful and formidable. If there is any country that can destroy North Korea, it is the U.S. Number two, they argue that given wartime operational control of South Korean forces by the U.S. that South Korea is nothing but a puppet of the U.S. Everything should be dealt with with the U.S. If the U.S. comes up with a peaceful arrangement with Pyongyang, South Korea will follow.

There's been a lot of attention on the new members of the National Assembly from the Democratic United Party and United Progressive Party who supposedly have pro–North Korea views. At the very least, many progressives simply refuse to criticize North Korea. Why do progressives who fought for human rights and democracy in South Korea seem to not fight for it in North Korea?

There are three elements. First, what [DUP chairman] Lee Hae-chan is saying is look at the July 4 joint communiqué and go back to basic agreement in 1992. Same with the June 15 declaration and October 4 declaration. The common understanding in all these agreements with North Korea is non-interference with domestic politics of each other, non-denunciation, no criticism. During the first Korean summit in 2000, both agreed not to engage in denunciation.

The second concern is the trade-off between basic human needs and human rights. Look at the Lee Myung-bak government. Because they raised the issue of North Korea human rights, who is suffering in North Korea? The ordinary citizens.

The third one is this: Lee Hae-chan and all others in the opposition party know we cannot force human rights and democracy in North Korea. The best way is opening and reform. Let North Korea have market mechanisms. Let North Korea have civil society. Let North Korea have a middle class. If we create the milieu within which North can easily take (the path of) opening and reform, the human rights condition will automatically improve.

Kim Dae-jung and Roh Moo-hyun were more concerned about human rights than Lee Myung-bak. What they were saying is what is the proper instrument to improve human rights? Let them achieve. We should provide the environment within which the North Korean people can achieve human rights and democracy.

The trade-off seems to be that if you don't talk about human rights, it looks like the dictatorship is getting a free pass to just keep acting in the worst way.

Doing is better than talking. The current government is nothing but talk. The previous two governments didn't speak out but brought up some changes. As a result of ten years of exchanges and cooperation, we have witnessed a lot of changes. They now worship money. Money has become so im-

South Korean President Kim Dae-jung

South Korean president Kim Dae-jung is often called the Nelson Mandela of Asia [after South African leader Nelson Mandela]. Beginning as a representative to the South Korean parliament from a rural province in 1960, Kim's voice championing real democracy and the end of military rule got louder and louder until he challenged the ruling president in 1971. After his defeat in the election, which some observers claim was rigged, he was almost murdered twice and then subjected to house arrest, imprisonment, torture, and a death sentence before the United States finally secured his release in 1982. After returning to Korea in 1985, he was put under house arrest again, but twice more tried to secure the presidency in 1987 and 1992. Kim was finally elected in 1997 and sworn into office in 1998. But his fight was just beginning, as commentators pointed out the nation's numerous problems that the new president would have to face. . . .

From June 13–15, 2000, Kim met with North Korean ruler Kim Jong-il; this was the first summit meeting between leaders of the two countries, which had been bitter rivals for 50 years. The two men signed an agreement in which they vowed to seek peace and reunification. They also agreed to allow visits between family members who had been separated by the two nations' border and to resolve other humanitarian issues.

Kim was awarded the Nobel Peace Prize on October 13, 2000. Praised for his moral strength, he was honored for his contribution to "democracy and human rights in South Korea and in East Asia in general, and for peace and reconciliation with North Korea in particular."

"Dae Jung Kim," Newsmakers:
Gale Biography in Context. Detroit: Gale, 1998.

portant in North Korea. That's partly because of exchange and cooperation. There has been a so-called newly emerging market mechanism.

In a planned society, money means nothing. But now, money has become very, very important. If you have improving basic human needs, eventually they will improve human rights. It's a matter of time.

Also, consider Asian politics. Face-saving is the most important thing. If we just say, 'You are a dictator' and at the same time 'Let us have a dialogue for peace,' how could it be possible?

Human rights groups and NGOs, they should talk about North Korea human rights. They should. And even the government should support. But the government should not lead. If you look at the human rights bill proposed by the ruling party, they can do nothing. They cannot affect human rights in North Korea. Conservative activists want to have their institutions and foundations funded, so they can get money.

So do you believe if South Korea keeps quiet about North Korea's human rights problems, North Korea will eventually improve?

The whole point is we are aware of human rights conditions in North Korea and we want improvement in human rights conditions in North Korea. But there is a method of improving human rights in North Korea. There is a priority too. For example, for me, peace is more important than human rights.

Basic human needs are more important than human rights. I know that human rights is a universal value we should strive towards. But peace is also a universal value. Satisfaction of basic human needs is a universal value. This is a priority problem.

If I were in the government, I would give more emphasis on peace and satisfaction of basic human needs, opening and reforming North Korea. And if human rights become an obstacle to those things, I would put it in the so-called lower category and let civil society lead on that.

North Korean leaders must realize that being open to South Korea will eventually bring problems for them. Why should they go along with engagement?

The peace offensive, North Koreans are aware of it, but it can be accompanied by an economic offensive that can benefit ordinary citizens. If I were North Korean leaders, yes, I know the trapping structure of the Sunshine Policy. But they cannot maintain their legitimacy without winning the hearts of North Korean citizens. North Korean leaders can create jobs, income and food for North Korean citizens. There is no reason for North Korean leaders to reject it, even though there could be a poison pill.

Our approach should be to say something like this to the North Korean leadership: 'I don't care about the North Korean dynasty. It's your problem. You could be like Deng Xiaoping. We want that kind of leader. But you could wind up like Ceausescu. That's your problem. For us, we want peace with you. We want economic cooperation. We will work hard to create a peaceful environment in which you can pursue that kind of project without worry and anxiety.'

In that process, we can get a lot of benefit, intentional and unintentional, including human rights and a democratic movement in North Korea.

Our approach should be to comfort the leader in such a way to derail the conservative forces from the military. It's a political game. North Korea knows, we know it. That is why we should not say, 'Oh your regime is bad.'

So what do you think are the chances for reviving the Sunshine Policy?

If the opposition party wins the upcoming election, the first thing they will do is restore peace with North Korea. Then, they will negotiate with North Korea. For them eventually they want democracy and a market in Korea. What they are saying is they have different methods. They don't want to politicize North Korea human rights for domestic purposes.

Even Park Geun-hye will do something different. If you read her article in *Foreign Affairs*, she suggested much more balanced diplomacy in the direction of multi-lateral cooperation. Of course, there is the [sunken warship] *Cheonan*. I don't know how she will handle that issue. I think she will resume the Mount Keumgang project and have a dialogue with North Korea.

What advice would you give to North Korea for getting what they want?

First of all, North Koreans would ask me, before I say anything to them, is your government going to treat our leader with respect? If I say yes, we will treat Kim Jong-eun with respect.

If that's the case, then I could say to North Korea, 'Calm yourself and don't play games. Go back to talks with the United States. Keep talking to China so you can resume the six-party talk process. If we have a new government in South Korea, don't show the old behavior. Congratulate the new government and then express your desire to have talks with South Korea. Try to show normal behavior. No more propaganda. Come forward with a straight voice.'

I have been telling North Koreans that. Very simple.

| "*The Sunshine Policy failed to produce the desired results the first time round because it never linked warmer relations with the North to progress on the nuclear issue, political liberalism or human rights conditions.*"

South Korea Should Not Return to the Sunshine Policy

John Hemmings

John Hemmings is a Sasakawa Peace Foundation fellow at Pacific Forum CSIS, a foreign policy research institute of the Center for Strategic and International Studies, in Honolulu, Hawaii. In the following viewpoint, he argues that South Korea's Sunshine Policy of fostering better relations with North Korea was not effective. He says that the Sunshine Policy was not linked to northern policy changes and that it assumed that economic liberalism would lead to political change. Hemmings argues that North Korea's militarism and ideology was too entrenched and that the Sunshine Policy merely made an untrustworthy regime stronger. He recommends against returning to the Sunshine Policy.

As you read, consider the following questions:

1. According to Hemmings, what arguments could be made in favor of the Sunshine Policy?

2. What does Hemmings say are problems caused by China's move toward open markets?

3. Why does Hemmings believe that the Sunshine Policy would reduce the likelihood of Korean reunification?

Some have speculated that South Korea's electorate, unhappy with [current president] Lee Myung-bak's handling of relations with North Korea, wants a return to [former presidents] Kim Dae-jung and Roh Moo-hyun's liberal policies—and with them, the Sunshine Policy, or greater engagement with Pyongyang [the capital of North Korea].

New Leader, New Policies

With [Kim Jong-un,] a new, young leader in power in North Korea [following the death of his father, Kim Jong-il], it would seem the right time to try something different—a new approach for a new era.

After all, the effectiveness of Lee's hard-line policy toward North Korea has increasingly been called into question. Tying inter-Korean relations to progress on the nuclear issue may have pleased Washington, but it quickly destroyed South Korea's developing relationship with the North. Since 2007, North Korea has shot a South Korean tourist, withdrawn from the Six-Party Talks [with the United States, China, Japan, Russia, and South Korea], tested another nuclear device, sunk a South Korean vessel and shelled civilians on an island in South Korea. If anything, it seems that Lee's policy has only raised inter-Korean tensions.

The Sunshine Policy would arguably bring North Korea back from teetering on the edge of financial collapse and enrich the state enough to feed its people. Instead of being backed into a corner, North Korea could follow China's path and enact financial reforms in select areas, which would benefit both the population and the country's neighbours. A wealthier North Korea would not feel so threatened, would not rely on threats and provocations to secure aid, and might even begin the long process of political liberalisation that so often accompanies economic reform.

All of this sounds very promising and hopeful, but it is unlikely to work. And even if it did, it could cause serious unintended consequences.

It Won't Work

There are two reasons for this. First, the Sunshine Policy failed to produce the desired results the first time round because it never linked warmer relations with the North to progress on the nuclear issue, political liberalism or human rights conditions. It therefore did not push North Korea to shift its own strategy. North-South ties became less acrimonious, but this arguably came at great cost to South Korea's security. While Seoul operated under Kim and Roh's liberal policies, the North continued to build up its military, withdrew from the Nuclear Non-Proliferation Treaty [officially the Treaty on the Non-Proliferation of Nuclear Weapons] (2003), tested a nuclear device (2006), continued research and development on its short-range and long-range missile program, and withdrew from the Six-Party Talks (2007). The cost-benefit ratio for symbolic goods was simply too high for the South.

Second, the Sunshine Policy rests on the false assumption that political liberalisation naturally follows on from market reforms. This may not always be true. Supporters of the Sunshine Policy often point to the success the West had in opening up Chinese markets, and the changes wrought on Chinese society since [Chinese Communist leader] Mao [Zedong]. This misses an important point: Is the region really better off now that China is rich? Certainly, it is a real achievement that

The Sunshine Policy and a Failure of Human Rights

To the North Korean people, victims of the most systematic totalitarian oppression in the modern world, [South Korean president] Kim Dae-jung offered no vision, no hope, and no future. When asked about human rights problems in North Korea at the American Enterprise Institute on March 8, 2001, three months after being awarded the Nobel Peace Prize, Kim Dae-jung said, "To affront North Korea with human rights issues in their face, with criticism, would not be wise—the greatest human rights issue on the Korean Peninsula is that of the 10 million members of the separated families." Such pronounced reluctance to address human rights issues set the tone for Kim Dae-jung's Sunshine era, which remained firmly in place throughout the term of his successor, Roh [Moo-hyun] despite rapidly expanding public information about North Korea's vast political-prisoner concentration camps and the inhumane conditions the North Korean state willfully maintained in those camps.

Sung-Yoon Lee, "Engaging North Korea: The Clouded Legacy of South Korea's Sunshine Policy," American Enterprise Institute, April 19, 2010.

so many Chinese people have been lifted from poverty, but a rising China has also presented the region with many new security challenges. States along China's coastline, including Vietnam, the Philippines and Japan, are now dealing with a bolder, more assertive China. This illustrates that there are unintended consequences to everything.

Do we really wish to enrich North Korea and give it the modern military that it thinks it deserves? Those who wish to rely on the liberal assumption are overlooking not only the unintended consequences, but also the fundamental nature of the regime. The Kim family derives its support from a uniquely Korean nationalist ideology, *Juche* (Self-reliance), adopted and upheld by the military. According to North Korea's highest-ranking defector, Hwang Jang-yop, the regime derives its support from the military, with the implicit promise that the state's ultimate purpose is to unify Korea. Would the regime jettison this belief simply because there was more money in the bank?

Sunshine and Reunification

Finally, this assumption overlooks the nature of the Korean situation. Large segments of the population in both North and South Korea still believe in reunification. But while a wealthier China was able to develop stronger economic ties with Taiwan, for example, it was also able to continue developing its missile arsenal across the Taiwan Strait. Similarly, a wealthier and militarily stronger Pyongyang would probably lessen any possibility of a Korean unification in the long run.

The Sunshine Policy is a good idea, based on a good principle. Unfortunately, it ignores the realities on the peninsula and the nature of the regime in the North, while also resting on a host of faulty assumptions.

| "*Any North Korean collapse and hurried reunification, analysts say, could spell the end of Pyongyang's ruling class while flooding Seoul with refugees and causing huge financial burdens.*"

Korea Reunification Would Spell Trouble for Seoul

Foster Klug

Foster Klug is the Associated Press news editor in Seoul, South Korea. In the following viewpoint, he reports that reunification of North and South Korea could be traumatic for both countries. In South Korea, hurried reunification could cause a flood of refugees from the North and massive economic destabilization. For the North itself, Klug says, reunification would probably help most North Koreans but would result in massive instability among elites, who would lose power and influence as well as face possible prosecution. Klug concludes that, despite the recent death of leader Kim Jong-il, reunification is unlikely to happen soon, which, he says, may be best for North and South Korea alike.

As you read, consider the following questions:

1. In what ways does North Korea's vision of reunification differ from South Korea's, according to Klug?

Foster Klug, "Korea Reunification Would Spell Trouble for Seoul," *The Huffington Post*, January 4, 2012.

2. What does Klug say are some differences between German reunification and potential Korean reunification?

3. What benefits does Klug suggest reunification might offer to South Korea's economy?

A single, reunified Korea has long been a cherished dream of people on both sides of the world's most heavily fortified border. South Korea even has a cabinet-level ministry preparing for the day.

And while Kim Jong Il's death last month has raised those hopes higher among some in Seoul, few are eager to talk about the cold reality: Sudden reunification could be traumatic for both countries.

Any North Korean collapse and hurried reunification, analysts say, could spell the end of Pyongyang's ruling class while flooding Seoul with refugees and causing huge financial burdens—perhaps trillions of dollars—for South Koreans who have only recently gotten used to their country's emergence as a rising Asian power.

Korea observers aren't predicting such a collapse or the kind of "big bang" reunification that happened in Germany, which saw the overnight fall of the Communist side and its swift absorption into its Western neighbor. The new North Korean leader, Kim Jong Il's son Kim Jong Un, is fast consolidating power, winning key backing from the government and military.

Still, the extraordinary changes in North Korea following the Dec. 17 death of the man whose iron rule lasted 17 years have stirred up dreams of a single Korea among some in the South. And not just in those with memories of life before the country was divided into U.S.- and Soviet-occupied zones in 1945.

The Swiss-educated Kim Jong Un "is less allergic than his father was to introducing new ideas from the world. That will help ease isolation and open room for reunification," said Bae

Sang-il, a 36-year-old office worker. "A generational change is meaningful in North Korea."

Many South Koreans support the idea of eventual reunification, but they seem more wary of the huge costs that will come with it.

A poll in South Korea late last year, before Kim's death, showed just over half of those interviewed believed they would eventually be better off after reunification, although more than two-thirds said the costs are bigger than the benefits.

Both countries talk about reunification, but they have very different notions of what it would be.

North Korea sees it as a two-state federation, with each state abiding by its own rules and regulations but as one Korea.

South Korea and its U.S. ally would likely balk at anything other than a Korea that's a liberal democracy, or at least moving in that direction.

From Seoul's point of view, slow and steady are crucial for any successful reunification. A sudden reunification would be a serious blow for South Korea's vibrant economy and well-ordered society.

South Korea, whose constitution enshrines the goal of reunification, will be much better off, analysts say, if it can gradually build up a North Korean economy that Seoul estimates is about one-fortieth its own size.

Officials in Seoul will be faced with a monumental set of problems, whatever happens. They will likely have to open up the North's economy to trade and investment, quickly raise the living standards of millions, control the flow of North Koreans into the South, and retrain North Korean bureaucrats so they can help run the country under new policies.

This will be very expensive.

A South Korean government-affiliated institute said recently that the cost could be up to $240 billion after a year and up to $2.4 trillion after a decade.

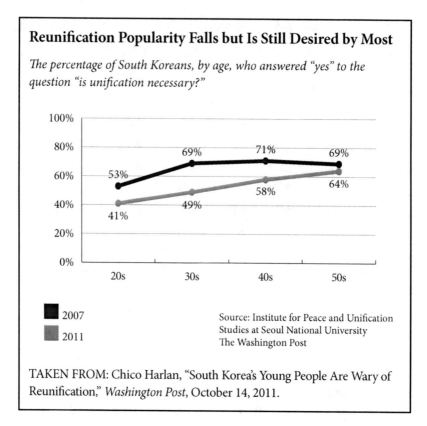

Reunification Popularity Falls but Is Still Desired by Most

The percentage of South Koreans, by age, who answered "yes" to the question "is unification necessary?"

2007
2011

Source: Institute for Peace and Unification Studies at Seoul National University
The Washington Post

TAKEN FROM: Chico Harlan, "South Korea's Young People Are Wary of Reunification," *Washington Post*, October 14, 2011.

South Korea's president has urged his country to prepare for reunification by studying the possibility of adopting a tax aimed at raising money for the costs of integration. The idea has largely stalled for the time being.

The German model is often raised for Korea, but there are important differences.

Germans in the West largely footed the bill for reunification after the collapse of communism, bringing the overall infrastructure of the former East Germany up to a standard similar to that in the West.

North Korea's population, however, is about half the size of the South's, while East Germany's population was only a quarter of the West's, according to Erik Lueth, an economist at the Royal Bank of Scotland. East Germany, he points out, was one of the wealthiest of the Soviet-affiliated states; North Korea is much poorer than the South, and there are estimates of widespread malnutrition.

Also, East Germany's ruling elite, chafing under the Soviet yoke, was not averse to the idea of uniting with West Germany and even accepting its capitalist system. North Korean leaders, analysts say, won't quickly accept a system that would take away their power and seek accountability for a rule that the United States and others say often trampled on rights.

"Reunification would be terrible for North Korea's elite and wonderful for the North Korean people, although there would be a traumatic period of adjustment," said Ralph Cossa, president of Pacific Forum CSIS, a Hawaii-based think tank. "For the top handful of North Korean leaders, reunification under Seoul would mean jail or worse."

For South Korea, reunification "will no doubt be messy and costly, even if it comes with a whimper, not a bang," Cossa said. Still, "living with a hostile, unpredictable, nuclear-armed North Korea is not much fun either."

Reunification could also provide eventual benefits for the South's economy.

Economist Marcus Noland at the Peterson Institute for International Economics describes a "peace dividend" that would come with a reduction in military tensions and the associated drop in military spending this would allow. The North also has abundant natural resources and a relatively well-educated and cheap labor force.

Predicting the future is, of course, a gamble, especially in a place as unpredictable as North Korea. That hasn't stopped people from trying: Paddy Power, an Irish betting agency, is offering odds of 12 to 1 that Korean reunification occurs before 2020.

History, however, provides some potential clues about North Korea's future. Despite famine, international isolation and outside skepticism, North Korea survived the 1994 death of Kim Il Sung, the North's founder and father of Kim Jong Il.

"Now, despite a food shortage and economic hardships, the regime will probably be able to avoid a worst-case scenario due to unity among its top officials and assistance from China," former South Korean Foreign Minister Han Sung-joo wrote recently in the *Chosun Ilbo*.

So reunification, at least for the time being, seems a distant dream. And that may be a good thing for Seoul.

> "Although the Chinese find little to love
> in North Korea, they prefer to prop it
> up, rather than see a takeover by South
> Korea that would bring US influence to
> the banks of the Yalu River."

Dear Leader's Big Moment for Détente?

Isabel Hilton

Isabel Hilton is editor of Chinadialogue.net. In the following viewpoint, she argues that reunification of South Korea and North Korea could move the united country in the direction of capitalism, democracy, and US interests. However, this would be contrary to the interests of China; therefore, China supports the North Korean regime and works to oppose reunification. Hilton also argues that the Bush era "axis of evil" attitude toward North Korea keeps North Korea on the defensive and belligerent, which also tends to work against reunification.

As you read, consider the following questions:

1. What countries would be party to talks about North Korea's nuclear program, according to the author?

2. What policy should the United States adopt toward North Korea in place of the George W. Bush strategy, according to the author?

3. What are the diplomatic ambitions of North Korea, according to the author?

Negotiating with North Korea was never simple—but as threats of confrontation with the South ease, signs are emerging that the tensions in the Korean Peninsula are beginning to subside after months of noisy confrontation. On 7 September the North released the captured seven-man crew of a South Korean fishing boat; days later, it proposed the resumption of a family reunion programme that has been suspended for longer than a year. Seoul, swallowing its distress at Pyongyang's sinking of its naval vessel the *Cheonan* in March, with the loss of 46 South Korean lives, is giving sympathetic consideration to North Korea's request for aid.

Meanwhile, Washington is pushing for resumption of the Six-Party Talks on the North's nuclear programme, involving China, Japan, the Koreas, Russia and the US. And a rumoured party conference this month is expected to reveal who will be the next leader of the world's most notorious pariah state. But there is unlikely to be any progress unless Washington, in particular, learns from past mistakes.

North Korea's Dear Leader, Kim Jong-il, is in poor health, and preparations for the coronation of his son Kim Jong-un have prompted speculation that the transition might push the cash-strapped regime to collapse. Pyongyang recently offered to repay its debt to the Czech Republic in kind—2,000 tonnes of ginseng, which, at current rates of consumption, would keep the Czechs going for 200 years. But North Korea has seen worse times: The last transition happened in 1994, when it was suffering a savage famine. Even so, the regime retained its grip. Its legitimacy, such as it is, rests on a narrative of patriotism and defiance that feeds on internal hardship and external hostility.

The escalation of economic sanctions by the US secretary of state, Hillary Clinton, is a sign that, in Washington, the diplomatic cupboard is bare. Despite decades of isolation and sanctions, North Korea remains a potentially dangerous nuclear state capable of attacking Tokyo and destroying Seoul. The military shadow-boxing of the past few months is nature's way of reminding us that the world's last cold war stand-off remains a potential flashpoint.

Efforts to resolve this stale confrontation are constrained by domestic politics on all fronts: In Washington, right-wing politicians are hostile to the suggestion that any deal is possible with an "axis of evil" state, and Pyongyang uses US hostility to justify its belligerence and excuse its failures. The US, North Korea and South Korea all proclaim unification as the ideal outcome for the divided peninsula, but none can produce an acceptable scenario to achieve it.

Reunification is the Augustinian goal of both Koreas—an outcome to be invoked, but not to be achieved any time soon. In Washington, regime collapse in the North is portrayed as the prelude to reunification along the lines of the German model, in which the capitalist South would absorb the discredited Communist state. This is the storybook ending, after all, to evil regimes. But China, Pyongyang's only friend, would not allow that to happen.

There is little affection these days between Beijing and Pyongyang. The North Korean regime is a truculent and unpredictable neighbour that both depends on and fears Beijing's power. Pyongyang takes care to set limits on Beijing's influence. But although the Chinese find little to love in North Korea, they prefer to prop it up, rather than see a takeover by South Korea that would bring US influence to the banks of the Yalu River, on the frontier between China and North Korea.

Half a century ago, China fought US-led troops in Korea back to the 38th parallel to prevent hostile forces from camping on its border. Today, it props up the Kim dynasty for the same reason. Dismal though North Korea's daily reality is, the status quo, for China, is the best achievable option.

New Rhetoric

Given Beijing's strategic imperatives, what can the US do? First, it should abandon the festering corpse of George W. Bush's "axis of evil" rhetoric and return to an era in which Washington had a sensible North Korea policy. In 1994, on President Bill Clinton's watch, a deal was struck in which North Korea promised to freeze and eventually dismantle its plutonium-producing nuclear facilities. In return, the US offered to supply 500,000 tonnes of heavy fuel oil a year, while Japan and South Korea pledged to build light-water reactors to address North Korea's severe energy shortage.

Had it come to fruition, North Korea would have had enough energy to revive its economy and Japan and South Korea could have escaped the threat—never to be discounted—that the North's nuclear capability might one day lead to a live war that nobody wants. But, in 2002, Bush accused North Korea of violating the deal. North Korea expelled the nuclear inspectors, fired up the Yongbyon reactor and reverted to a policy of threat. From Pyongyang's perspective at least, it works.

North Korea has a few, relatively straightforward, diplomatic ambitions: a peace treaty, normalisation of relations with the US and some version of the aborted Clinton agreement. If that could be achieved, long-suffering North Koreans could aspire to modest prosperity and a less paranoid state. China's security concerns would be addressed, Japan could sleep more easily, and a more stable North Korea might become a possible partner for eventual reunification. Now that the other options have failed, perhaps the lessons can be learned.

> *"Those abducted include not just Japanese and South Koreans (nearly 500 of whom have been taken over the course of half a century) but Lebanese, Thais, Malaysians, Chinese and allegedly— Dutch, French and Italians as well."*

Lost, Without a Trace

Hideko Takayama and Evan Thomas

Hideko Takayama is a journalist who has contributed to Newsweek, and Evan Thomas has been a managing editor at Newsweek. In the following viewpoint, they discuss the hardships that the North Korean program of abduction of so many foreign nationals has caused. The authors describe the beginnings of the abduction program after the Korean War that focused on South Koreans and the escalation of the program in the 1970s to foreign nationals from virtually any country as part of a spy-training campaign. The authors explain that one country with many victims of the program is Japan, which threatens to withhold war reparations from North Korea until the abductee issue is resolved.

As you read, consider the following questions:

1. When and in what circumstances do the authors say that Kim Jong Il admitted the existence of an abduction program?

2. What role did the abductees play in the spy-training program of North Korea, according to the authors?

3. What sum do the authors say Japan might pay in reparations for the Japanese occupation of Korea during World War II if North Korea would settle the abductee issue?

The 13-year-old girl was on her way home from badminton practice when she disappeared. Every night for five years, her mother kept the porch light on, hoping against hope for Megumi Yokota's return. That was almost 30 years ago. Then in 1996, Sakie Yokota and her husband learned that the North Koreans had snatched their daughter as part of a bizarre abduction program that had kidnapped scores of Japanese, perhaps as many as a hundred, in the 1970s and '80s.

Ever since, Megumi Yokota's story has been a sensation in the Japanese press. In 2002, North Korea's leader, Kim Jong Il, admitted to Japanese Prime Minister Junichiro Koizumi that North Korean agents had been abducting Japanese nationals. The ruler of the Hermit Kingdom offered, along with his apologies, a list of eight Japanese who North Korea claimed had died in captivity and five who were still living. The Yokotas were initially informed that Megumi had committed suicide in 1993; the elderly couple was handed a jar supposedly containing their daughter's ashes. But DNA tests showed that the remains belonged to two different people—neither of them Megumi. "I feel like I'm going to explode. How long do I have to endure this pain?" asks Sakie Yokota, now 70.

Possibly as long as the twisted, repressive North Korean regime lasts. The Dear Leader is not known for heeding humanitarian concerns. Still, the pressure is on Pyongyang. Last week Japanese and North Korean representatives met in Beijing to discuss "normalizing" relations between the two countries. High on the agenda: North Korea's nuclear program and the case of the missing abductees. (At the talks, Pyongyang bizarrely insisted that Tokyo hand over seven human rights activists in Japan, calling them "criminal abductors of North Korean nationals.") In December, the United Nations adopted a resolution criticizing North Korea's human rights record, including the abduction program. In the same month, a pair of Japanese support groups hosted a meeting of the families of kidnap victims that revealed how widely North Korean agents had ranged the globe looking for prey. Those abducted include not just Japanese and South Koreans (nearly 500 of whom have been taken over the course of half a century) but Lebanese, Thais, Malaysians, Chinese and allegedly—Dutch, French and Italians as well. The stories that are coming out about Pyongyang's body snatchers would make for a spy movie—a very tragic one.

The motivations of North Korea's rulers are often murky, but apparently Pyongyang geared up its abduction program to train better spies. In the mid-1970s, when his father, Kim Il Sung, was still alive, Kim Jong Il was in charge of espionage operations. He decided that North Korea's spies needed to look, dress and act like capitalists in order to blend in with their targets. The North Koreans were already in the kidnapping business by then. They had been snatching South Koreans ever since the end of the Korean War in 1953. In 1969, a South Korean airliner was hijacked and flown to Wonsan, a city across the DMZ. Pyongyang agreed to repatriate 39 people, but 11 South Koreans were held back—and have never returned.

Starting in 1977, North Korean agents were "ordered to bring foreign nationals in *magjabi* [a Korean term meaning 'grab anybody']," says Tsutomu Nishioka, vice president of the

National Association for the Rescue of Japanese Kidnapped by North Korea (NARKN), who has interviewed former North Korean agents. Many were put to work as cultural trainers for North Korean spies in an elaborate stage set built in a huge tunnel beneath Pyongyang. According to a book written by Ahn Myong Jin, a former North Korean agent who defected to the South in 1993, "There were re-created examples of South Korean supermarkets, banks, high-class hotels, a night district, police stations, and elementary and middle schools." Ahn recalled "more than 80 people who trained us to become 'South Koreans.' Most of them were abducted from the South to be used as our teachers." Ahn said that the South Koreans he met "all seemed to have deep pain inside their heart. One teacher who taught us how to behave at drinking joints in the South said, 'You are sneaking into the South, but please do not bring [back] innocent South Korean children playing on the beach.'"

The eccentric and sybaritic Jong Il was interested in more than better-trained spies. "He is a collector of human species," says Cho Gab Je, a leading South Korean journalist. A movie buff, Kim instructed his agents to snatch a famous South Korean actress, Choi Un-hee, and her husband, movie director Shin Sang-ok. Abducted from Hong Kong in 1978, Choi and Shin escaped to the West in 1986 and produced a remarkable book, *The Echo from Darkness*. Among their recollections was an encounter with a Chinese woman who described how she had been abducted in Macau. Two men, pretending to be scions of wealthy Japanese families, appeared in the jewelry store where the woman was working. They lured her out on a boat ride—and then to a larger ship that whisked her off to North Korea. Choi also heard a sad tale in Pyongyang about a French woman. She claimed that she had been seduced by a good-looking North Korean agent who took her to meet his parents in Pyongyang. There, the agent vanished and the woman— yelling in protest—was taken away.

The North Korean agents enticed other victims with promises of work. Four Lebanese women were abducted in 1978 by agents posing as Japanese who visited a secretarial school in Beirut. The men offered the women well-paying jobs in Japanese corporations—and spirited them off to Pyongyang. After the Lebanese government and their families protested, the women were released in 1979. But one, who had already married a U.S. Army deserter and was pregnant, went back to North Korea. Her mother, Mountaha Haidar, is bereft. She was allowed to visit her daughter once in Pyongyang (but not to go to her home) and she receives one call a year. Her daughter is always guarded on the phone, asking only about her mother's well-being. Says Haidar: "North Korea destroyed the life of my daughter." Some of the Lebanese victims reportedly testified in 1979 that they were trained to become spies along with three French, two Dutch and three Italian women.

Stories of abductees are still surfacing. Last November, in the northern Thai village of Nong Sae, outside the city of Chiang Mai, Sukham Panjoy and his son Banjong were idly watching the news on TV before dinner. Conversation suddenly stopped when they heard that a Thai woman who had disappeared from Macau in 1978 was alive and living in Pyongyang. Her name was Anocha, and she was Sukham Panjoy's long-lost younger sister. "I was so happy, but then I was suddenly angry that she was taken," says Sukham. "Since she's disappeared, I've never been the same."

The Panjoys were flown by two of the abductee support groups to Tokyo, where they met the source of their good news: Charles Robert Jenkins, a U.S. Army deserter who had spent nearly 40 years in North Korea. Now living in Japan, Jenkins says he had been Anocha's neighbor in Pyongyang. Like many poor young women, Anocha had moved to Bangkok looking for employment in the 1970s. In 1977, she apparently went to work in Macau in a massage parlor. ("She was always very pretty," says her nephew Banjong, as he laid out her pictures for a *Newsweek* reporter in the family farmhouse.) Abducted by the North Koreans, she was married off to another American Army deserter. Jenkins told the Panjoy family that Anocha had learned to speak English, enjoyed gardening and remained relatively happy.

The North Korean government has denied kidnapping Anocha and says she's not in the country. But the Thai government is pressing, and Pyongyang may not be able to stonewall forever. The perpetually cash-strapped North Korean government has a financial incentive to come clean. Lately, the U.S. Treasury Department has been pressuring banks in Macau suspected of laundering money for Kim Jong Il. Pyongyang fears that Washington will zero in on Kim's secret bank accounts in other countries, including Switzerland.

Desperate for money, North Korea is eager to normalize ties with Japan. One big reason: Japan has indicated that it will pay Pyongyang about $10 billion as compensation for the Japanese occupation of Korea from 1910 to 1945. But, warns Shinzo Abe, Japan's hawkish chief cabinet secretary, "Without solving the abductees' case, Japan will not conclude the normalization talks."

Japan has other demands. Pyongyang holds some 1,800 Japanese wives of former North Korean residents who have followed their husbands into the Hermit Kingdom. And Tokyo wants Pyongyang to hand over Shin Kwang Soo, a big-time North Korean spy who is believed responsible for several abduction cases. One of them was little Megumi Yokota. Sakie Yokota clings to the hope that her daughter is still alive. After an abductee victim returning to Japan claimed that he saw Megumi Yokota still alive in 1994, the North Koreans changed Megumi's date of death from March 1993 to April 1994. It is certain that Megumi had a daughter, who still lives in North Korea. Sakie Yokota still dreams of the day when she can see both her daughter and granddaughter.

> *"The strength of feelings about pan-*
> *Korean nationalism makes progressive*
> *and even many conservative [South*
> *Korean] politicians reluctant to touch*
> *the issue [of North Korean abduc-*
> *tions]."*

South Korea's Response to North Korean Abductions Is Politicized and Inadequate

Brad Williams and Erik Mobrand

Brad Williams and Erik Mobrand are both visiting fellows in the Department of Political Science at the National University of Singapore. In the following viewpoint, the authors argue that in both Japan and South Korea, the issue of North Korean abductions of foreign nationals has become tied to nationalism. In Japan, they say, this has led to a hard line against North Korea. In South Korea, however, visions of a unified Korea have made South Korean politicians unwilling to push North Korea on the issue of abductions. In both cases, the authors say, the politicization of the issue has interfered with the priority of protecting and rescuing those who were kidnapped.

Brad Williams and Erik Mobrand, "Explaining Divergent Responses to the North Korean Abductions Issue in Japan and South Korea," *Journal of Asia Studies*, vol. 69, no. 2, May 2010, pp. 507–510, 521–524, 531–533. Copyright © 2010 The Association for Asian Studies, Inc. Reprinted with the permission of Cambridge University Press.

As you read, consider the following questions:

1. According to the authors, how many Japanese and South Korean nationals are thought to be detained in North Korea?

2. Why do the authors say that South Korea chose to redefine abductees as members of separated families in negotiations with North Korea?

3. What are South Koreans torn between in the Sunshine era, according to the viewpoint?

This [viewpoint] examines the divergent approaches pursued by Japan and South Korea in their attempts to resolve an issue that is related to a fundamental responsibility of sovereign states: the protection of citizens. The case considered here is North Korea's abduction of Japanese and South Korean nationals. In Japan, the abduction issue has taken center stage in the country's North Korea policy, whereas in South Korea, recent administrations have downplayed the issue—despite the fact that nearly 500 South Korean citizens remain detained in North Korea, compared to fewer than 20 known Japanese abductions. The authors find that the key to understanding the divergent responses lies in the politicization of specific, ostensibly apolitical demands for the state to fulfill its duty to protect citizens. In particular, the proximity of the abductions issue to key nationalist themes, which politicians in each country use to mobilize support, prevents the matter from being addressed in a neutral way.

Firm Diplomacy vs. Quiet Diplomacy

It is now well known that the North Korean government has in past decades engaged in the abduction of foreign nationals, notably from neighbors Japan and South Korea. While it would be expected that any responsible government would pursue the repatriation of its citizens who have disappeared abroad, Japan and South Korea have reacted in opposite ways. In Japan, the government has remained committed to negotiating "firmly" (*gizen to*) on the abductions issue, so that it has taken center stage in the country's North Korea policy, even to the point of freezing Japan out of regional efforts to resolve the North Korean nuclear crisis. In South Korea, however, recent administrations have downplayed the abductions issue, instead following a policy of "quiet diplomacy" (*choyonghan woegyo*). The contrasting responses are all the more surprising given that nearly 500 South Korean citizens remain detained in North Korea, compared to fewer than 20 known abductions from Japan. What accounts for the different approaches to this issue in Japan and South Korea—both U.S. allies that share democratic commitments?

The key to understanding the divergent responses to the abductions lies in the politicization of specific, ostensibly apolitical demands for the state to fulfill its core duty to protect citizens. In neither Japan nor South Korea has the abductions issue made its way into public debate as only a problem of protecting citizens. Instead, the maneuverings of political actors in both countries have made it inseparable from broader agendas. In particular, the proximity of the abductions issue to key nationalist themes, which politicians in each country use to mobilize support, prevents the matter from being addressed in a neutral way. In Japan, the issue easily generates sympathy for the right-wing agenda of restoring Japan to the status of "normal" nation [that is, without the restrictions on military action imposed after World War II], and it is therefore quickly seized upon by political actors with that agenda. In South Korea, the issue inevitably raises questions about ongoing reconciliation with North Korea. Some politicians who push for a tougher stance on North Korea embrace the issue, while most who favor reconciliation suppress it. The strength of feelings about pan-Korean nationalism makes progressive and even many conservative politicians reluctant to touch the issue. The forces politicizing the issue are strong enough to push Japan to the point of undermining its own national interest in participating in efforts at regional cooperation, and in South Korea, to drive away public debate on the issue. . . .

Genesis of the Abductions

North Korean plans to abduct Japanese citizens were first devised in the mid-1970s. The Japanese abductions were a by-product of the failed assassination attempt on South Korean president Park Chung-hee in August 1974. The would-be assassin, Mun Se-gwang, was an ethnic Korean resident of Japan (Zainichi) and a sympathizer of the North Korean regime. In the aftermath of this incident, the South Korean government initiated a more thorough program of background checks on Zainichi Koreans seeking entry into the country and strengthened security measures against North Korean spies. The North Korean intelligence community was forced to look elsewhere for recruits and began targeting Japanese citizens in order to steal their identities and educate their own agents in the subtleties of Japanese language and culture to facilitate this process.

The first suspected North Korean abduction of a Japanese national was that of Kume Yutaka, a fifty-two-year-old security guard who disappeared near the coast in Ishikawa Prefecture in September 1977. This marked the beginning of a six-year period in which another sixteen Japanese citizens vanished under mysterious circumstances. The abductees fell under three broad categories: (1) individuals, some of whom may have been deliberately targeted . . . , (2) couples on dates and (3) Japanese in Europe. The three Japanese travelers in Europe were lured to North Korea by Japanese women who themselves had previously been enticed to the Stalinist state to marry members of Japan's Red Army Faction (*Sekigunha*), which was responsible for the hijacking of a Japanese airliner in 1970. While relatives and a few supporters had their suspicions, the circumstances surrounding the missing Japanese would remain shrouded in mystery for more than two decades.

The situation of South Korean citizens taken and detained in North Korea is quite different from those from Japan. Most of the South Korean cases occurred more than three decades ago, and in fact, only twenty-four of those still missing were taken after the first suspected kidnapping of a Japanese [citizen] in 1977. For the purposes of this [viewpoint], we are concerned only with South Koreans who were detained in the DPRK [that is, the Democratic People's Republic of Korea, or North Korea] at some point after the Korean War. This definition excludes prisoners of war (POWs) as well as the tens of thousands of South Korean civilians who were taken North during the war. Since the 1953 armistice, 3,790 Republic of Korea (ROK) [South Korea] citizens are believed to have been detained in North Korea against their wishes. Most were returned, but 485 abductees are thought to remain in North Korea. Some may have been taken to be trained as spies.

The vast majority of abductees—433 of the remaining 485—were fishermen. In many cases, the DPRK asserted that their ships had crossed over into North Korean waters. In 1969, North Koreans hijacked a Korean Air flight with fifty-one people on board, of whom twelve remain in North Korea. The following year, twenty South Koreans were taken from a naval ship. The kidnappings most reminiscent of the Japanese cases involved five high school students who disappeared from a remote coastal area in 1977 and 1978, and who were known only by the late 1990s to have been taken by the DPRK. Finally, several ROK citizens were kidnapped overseas, including in West Germany, Norway, and China, and twelve of these abductees remain in the North. It is likely that the actual number of South Koreans detained in North Korea is higher than that recorded. Four former abductees have returned to South Korea, and one of these, Kim Pyŏng-do, was not on the list of known missing people.

According to the DPRK government, no South Korean citizens have been taken against their will. As a DPRK newspaper put it, "Even if there are people who have entered North Korea [*ippukcha*], there are no abductees [*nappukcha*]." In South Korea, the issue is further complicated by the possibility that the ROK government itself kidnapped North Korean citizens. At least until the 1990s, the South Korean government was equally suspicious of Koreans with contacts on both sides of the demilitarized zone. Alleged spies from North Korea were, of course, detained in South Korea. That South Korean authorities have never acknowledged taking North Korean citizens is by no means solid evidence that it was only the North that engaged in this type of activity. . . .

South Korean Reconciliation with the North: From Reciprocity to "Quiet Diplomacy"

The detainment of citizens by North Korea has been known for decades. Since the early 1970s, the abductions have arisen periodically as an issue in inter-Korean relations. The state of North-South relations and domestic politics in South Korea prevented any movement for the return of abductees from developing until much later. The ROK had very little communication with the DPRK and no room for negotiating the return of detained citizens. Furthermore, South Korea was run by authoritarian leaders who, far from fighting for the rights of citizens, committed atrocities against their own people. In that context, there would have been no political space within South Korea until at least the late 1980s, if not later, for families of abductees to press for more attention to the problem of kidnappings by North Korea.

Early efforts to resolve the abductions issue were spearheaded by the South Korean National Red Cross (KNRC), which achieved short-lived breakthroughs in 1972–73 and 1985. These efforts were couched within the broader framework of family reunions, a perennial topic in inter-Korean relations. The purpose of the joint Red Cross talks held in 1972–73 was to find a way of pursuing the shared goal of collecting information on separated family members: learning whether family members were alive and, if so, where they lived. Very little came of the talks before they broke down in 1973, not to be resumed for another twelve years. In 1985, both the North and South Red Crosses agreed to search for a permanent reunion of separated families—an ambitious goal. The negotiations stumbled along and claimed something of a success when brief reunions of separated family members (and an exchange of artistic troupes) were held. No progress specifically on the abductions issue was made, and in January 1986, the DPRK cited the ROK's Team Spirit exercises with the United States as the reason for cutting contact with the South. North Korea's endeavors to discredit the upcoming 1988 Seoul Olympic Games meant that relations did not improve again for some time. Still, the 1985 reunions were unprecedented and served as a model when reunions were resumed fifteen years later.

In the 1990s, the abductions issue gained public attention in South Korea at a few points in time in response to new information and in debates over what to do with former North Korean spies. In August 1994, Amnesty International released a report revealing that at least forty-nine South Koreans taken by North Korea were being held in prison camps in the North, prompting the families of three abductees to appeal to the KNRC for help. Also in the 1990s, several convicted North Korean spies were completing their prison terms, and the DPRK demanded their repatriation. Seoul's policy in these cases was to insist on the principle of reciprocity: a North Korean prisoner would be returned if the DPRK returned an imprisoned or kidnapped ROK citizen. In 1992, Pyongyang rejected such a deal when it demanded the return of former spy Yi In-mo, who himself wanted to be repatriated, and went further to cancel a planned round of family exchanges. A year later, to the chagrin of many in the South, Yi was sent home, but no South Korean was released in return.

More information about South Koreans detained in the North became available in part because of greater contact across the demilitarized zone, but also because of knowledge brought by North Koreans fleeing famine for China and eventually other countries. In December 1997, the South Korean defense ministry confirmed the existence of some 100 POWs in the North, and in early 1999, the government released a list of 454 known living abductees as well as 231 POWs. Longtime activist Kim Dae-jung had taken office in 1998, and he worked to act on the new information. In early 1999, his administration offered to repatriate North Korean prisoners, as long as the North released the living POWs and abductees. Many former DPRK spies were released on amnesty and desired to be returned to the North. Pyongyang rejected the offer, claiming that no ROK citizens were being held against their will in the North. Exchanging citizens appeared to be the best option on the table for addressing the problem, but because of the DPRK's refusal to recognize that the country was holding South Koreans, the approach did not help the South Korean government make progress on the abductions issue.

Sunshine and Kim Dae-jung

Through his Sunshine Policy, President Kim Dae-jung sought to initiate reconciliation with the North and improve inter-Korean relations. The breakthrough came with the North-South joint summit held in Pyongyang on June 15, 2000, at which Kim Jong Il and Kim Dae-jung met and signed an agreement. The summit set the stage for family reunions as well as economic exchange between the Koreas. The abductions issue was not addressed at the summit.

Percentage of the Japanese Public That Knows About the North Korean Abductions

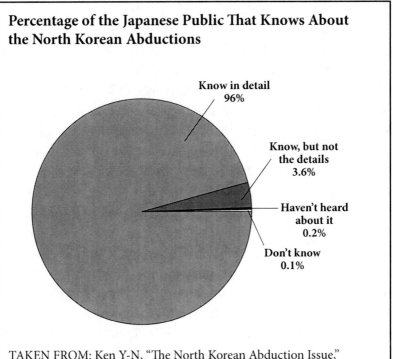

Know in detail
96%

Know, but not
the details
3.6%

Haven't heard
about it
0.2%

Don't know
0.1%

TAKEN FROM: Ken Y-N, "The North Korean Abduction Issue," *What Japan Thinks,* July 26, 2012. whatjapanthinks.com.

In the aftermath of the historic June summit, there was much excitement in South Korea about the possibilities for greater contact with North Korea. The South Korean administration decided that it would act on earlier plans to repatriate sixty-three former North Korean spies. Detractors were furious about the plan and about other acts of generosity to the DPRK. In early September, South Korea released the former spies without demanding that South Korean citizens be released in return. The moment was a watershed. Until then, the administration had promised repatriation of the North Koreans only on the condition of the North returning ROK citizens. The families of abductees were outraged, and years later, they continue to see that act as the point at which the ROK government was no longer negotiating with North Korea but groveling at Kim Jong Il's feet.

At stake was the principle of reciprocity (*sangho chuŭi*). President Kim was criticized for abandoning that principle in dealings with the DPRK. In the weeks leading up to the repatriation and after, conservative editorials slammed the administration for the move. [South Korean daily newspaper] *Chosun Ilbo*, for example, declared, "No matter how important South-North reconciliation is, there cannot be 'reconciliation' in a way that smashes the foundation of the nation." The government responded that it had not abandoned reciprocity: Former spies were a Cold War issue, but POWs and other detainees were matters of state and security, and so could not be equated. Moreover, President Kim articulated a different vision of exchange with the DPRK, beyond a simple give-and-take relationship: "We are not going to apply the principle of reciprocity for humanitarian support in order for our North Korean brothers to escape hunger, but we are going to apply the principle of reciprocity for economic cooperation, including helping with North Korea's economic development and setting up enterprises." For President Kim, reconciliation meant approaching the DPRK with open arms, not making calculating deals.

Instead of reciprocity, by September 2000, President Kim's administration had embraced "quiet diplomacy" (*choyonghan woegyo*) as the approach to North Korea on sensitive issues such as abductees. The quiet approach avoids direct confrontation over the abductions issue in negotiations with North Korea. The key point is that the government redefined abductees, as well as POWs, as members of "separated families" (*yisan kajok*). An ROK white paper from 2001 explains the rationale behind this change: "Because the North is currently denying the existence of the abductees and POWs in North Korea, the ROK government believes it will not help matters to continue an unproductive discussion about their existence. The government is trying to solve this matter by including abductees and POWs in the category of separated families." By putting abductees in the category of separated families, the government gave the families of abductees some hope of meeting their kin, or at least learning more about them.

The first round of reunions took place in August 2000. In the second round, later in 2000, a former POW in the North was allowed to meet his brother from the South. In January 2001, the Red Cross pushed for more abductees and POWs to be included in reunions and allocated them and their relatives a portion of the space in delegations for family meetings. The administration and the Red Cross considered the deal a breakthrough, because explicit reference to South Koreans detained in the North was taken so poorly by DPRK representatives. Now families of abductees could at least be offered an opportunity to meet their relatives or gain information about their status and whereabouts. They have become included in the reunions as members of "special separated families" (*t'ŭksu yisan kajok*). In the next round of reunions, two POWs and an abducted flight attendant were included, and through those meetings, more was learned about other abductees. Two South Korean fishermen taken by DPRK authorities in 1987 were included in family reunions at North Korea's Mount Kumgang in September 2009.

The election of Lee Myung-bak, who became president in February 2008, raised the possibility of change in South Korea's approach to the abductions issue. Lee pledged to make efforts to solve the problem early in his tenure. Soon after he took office, the Ministry of Unification laid out a plan for dealing with the issue. Within the Ministry of Unification, Lee's administration has established an Abductee Support Directorate (*nappuk p'ihaeja chiwŏndan*), which is tasked with collecting information on possible abductees and assisting in the repatriation of those who are in third countries. Perhaps the most significant development is the inclusion of "special separated families" in the family reunions. Despite Lee's willingness to risk harming North-South relations, his administration has done little in its first two years to depart substantially from the "quiet diplomacy" approach on this issue. . . .

Nationalism and Abduction

The abductions issue is certainly a real one: The DPRK has admitted to kidnapping thirteen Japanese nationals, though it continues to deny holding further Japanese and South Koreans against their will. However, the responses from Japan and South Korea do not seem commensurate with the duties of states to protect their citizens. This [viewpoint] has shown how specific demands by the families of abductees have been overwhelmed by political actors who have framed the issue in terms of broader agendas. In both Japan and South Korea, the political environment has caused the abductions issue to become distorted and rarely presented in public debate as only a problem of protecting citizens. Rather, the issue becomes wrapped up in calls for restoration of Japan as a "normal" nation and debates over achieving pan-Korean solidarity.

Nationalism has been a factor in shaping how the issue plays out in both countries, but its role has been different in each case. Extremist elements in the Japanese repatriation movement have sought to instrumentalize the campaign in order to pursue a broad nationalist agenda, ensuring that the abductions issue retains a prominent place in Japan's North Korea diplomacy. Restorationist nationalism has made many Japanese especially sensitive to violations of sovereignty, a point that helps explain why conservative politicians have been successful in mobilizing popular support on the abductions issue. The ethnic nationalism that has swept South Korea has had the opposite effect on attitudes toward the abductions issue: An ideology of pan-Korean solidarity encourages South Koreans to put precisely these sorts of acts by North Korea behind them. In the Sunshine era, South Koreans are torn between seeking to heal old wounds on the Korean Peninsula and acknowledging that North Korea's political system does not square with the South's newly gained democratic sensibilities. Ethnic nationalism has helped push many South Koreans to prioritize reconciliation with the North while adhering to a selective silence when that goal conflicts with democratic values. . . .

Despite an administration in South Korea that is less interested in reconciliation with the North, major change on the abductions issue seems unlikely. Under Lee [Myung-bak], North-South relations have taken a turn for the worse without really benefiting anyone and without the ROK pushing the abductions issue. Furthermore, the administration appears unwilling to make the concessions necessary for progress on the issue to be achieved.

Periodical and Internet Sources Bibliography

The following articles have been selected to supplement the diverse views presented in this chapter.

Jong-Yun Bae	"South Korean Strategic Thinking Toward North Korea: The Evolution of the Engagement Policy and Its Impact upon U.S.-ROK Relations," *Asian Survey*, vol. 50, no. 2, March/April 2010, pp. 335–355.
Mark P. Barry	"Korean Reunification Would Cast Off China's Shadow," *World Policy Blog*, June 11, 2012.
CBC News	"South Korea Fires at North Korea Fishing Boats," September 21, 2012.
David Coghlan	"Prospects from Korean Reunification," Strategic Studies Institute, April 2008.
Daily Yomiuri	"North Korea Abduction Issue Still Haunts Govt," September 18, 2012.
John M. Glionna	"Korea Reunification: Is It a Dream or Could It Become Reality?," *Los Angeles Times*, December 20, 2011.
Donald Kirk	"South Korea Shirks from Abduction Issue," *Asia Times Online*, September 24, 2011.
Ronald Popeski	"Sunshine Policy Failed to Change North Korea: Report," Reuters, November 18, 2010.
VOA News	"South Korea Formally Declares End to Sunshine Policy," November 17, 2010.
Lucy Williamson	"New Report Highlights North Korean Abductions," BBC News, May 13, 2011.
Park Young-Ho and Kim Hyeong Ki	"2011 Unification Clock: When Will We See a Unified Korea?," Korea Institute for National Unification, December 2011.

OPPOSING
VIEWPOINTS®
SERIES

What Is the Relationship Between the Koreas and the World?

Chapter Preface

Korea and Japan have a long and contested history. At the beginning of the twentieth century, Japan annexed Korea. Then, during World War II, Japan conscripted Koreans and forced them to work under slave labor conditions. Hundreds of thousands died. In addition, the Japanese forced many Korean women to serve as sexual slaves for their armed forces during the war. These "comfort women" have become a rallying point for anti-Japanese sentiment in South Korea to the present day.

Despite their history of conflict, today South Korea and Japan are both democratic allies of the United States, and both share many national interests. As a result, efforts have been made to try to forge closer ties between the two countries. One of the most recent steps in this direction was a military pact between Japan and South Korea that would provide for greater sharing of intelligence between the two countries. In particular, the treaty would focus on what Choe Sang-Hun in a June 28, 2012, article called "two major common concerns: North Korea's nuclear and missile threats and China's growing military might."

However, while the United States pushed for the agreement, in South Korea it was massively politically unpopular, sparking protests and vociferous attacks on the government of President Lee Myung-bak. Opposition leaders and commenters warned that the treaty could lead to a resurgence of Japanese militarism. As a result, an hour before the official signing, scheduled in June 2012, the event was postponed, according to a June 29, 2012, article from BBC News. The South Korean government said that it was still interested in pushing the agreement forward, but progress has been stalled.

Ralph A. Cossa, in a July 2012 report from the Council on Foreign Relations, argues that the military pact would greatly facilitate military planning in the region. He suggests that the issue of Korean comfort women needs to be confronted and depoliticized so that the two nations can move forward, and he recommends the United States serve as a mediator to help "put this cancerous issue behind for the sake of both" Japan and Korea.

Many Koreans, however, do not see the issue in these terms. A July 1, 2012, editorial in the *Korea Times*, for example, links Japan's past actions to a current dispute between Japan and Korea over the Dokdo islands. The editorial states:

> "More than a century ago, Japan occupied these volcanic outcroppings in the body of water between the two nations, signaling the start of its scheme to colonize Korea. That Tokyo resumed its territorial claims over the rocky outlets a few decades ago indicates the country is not just refusing to repent on its historical wrongs but is even willing to repeat them all over if circumstances allow."

Thus, for many in Korea, Japan's past remains relevant to its current actions—and that makes military cooperation with Japan very unpopular in South Korea.

Besides their links to Japan, South and North Korea have numerous other international ties in East Asia and throughout the world. The remainder of this chapter looks at some of the most important of those relationships.

"It would be hard to create a policy toward North Korea that does more damage to Chinese national interests than Beijing's current approach to Pyongyang."

China's North Korea Policy Is Illogical and Damages Chinese Interests

Ralph A. Cossa and Brad Glosserman

Ralph A. Cossa is president and Brad Glosserman is executive director of Pacific Forum CSIS, a foreign policy research institute of the Center for Strategic and International Studies. In the following viewpoint, the authors argue that China's current policy toward North Korea damages China's own interests. Specifically, the authors say that by refusing to denounce North Korean aggressive actions or to put pressure on North Korea, China makes the region less stable. They argue that Chinese policy also antagonizes South Korea and pushes it toward Japan and the United States and away from China. The authors suggest that some Chinese policy makers realize that the current North Korea policy is counterproductive. They hope that a change in China's North Korea policy may come sooner rather than later.

Ralph A. Cossa and Brad Glosserman, "The Illogic of China's North Korea Policy," Pac-NET, no. 32, May 17, 2012. Copyright © 2012 by Pacific Forum CSIS. All rights reserved. Reproduced by permission.

As you read, consider the following questions:

1. What do the authors say is the standard explanation for China's policy toward North Korea?

2. According to the authors, how does China's policy contribute to the strengthening of the US alliance system?

3. What do the authors say about Korean reunification, and why is this a problem for China?

Discussions in Beijing about North Korea are always frustrating. It's not so much due to the sharp divergence in US and Chinese thinking about how to deal with Pyongyang [the capital of North Korea]; the two sides differ on many issues. No, the real problem is the illogic of the Chinese position—at least from a US perspective. Indeed, it would be hard to create a policy toward North Korea that does more damage to Chinese national interests than Beijing's current approach toward Pyongyang.

China Enables

The standard explanation for Chinese policy goes like this: While denuclearization is desired, stability comes first. There is little chance that North Korea can be persuaded to give up its weapons—at least for a long time—as its arsenal is seen as a form of legitimacy and a deterrent to regime change. Moreover, Beijing has limited influence in Pyongyang and North Korea's real aim is a relationship with the US, hopefully one that sidelines Seoul as well. This logic produces a policy of minimal pressure on Pyongyang, calls for good behavior by all parties, demands that the US soften its position and be more accommodative, and the fending off of demands for Beijing to do more to bring Pyongyang around.

Recent discussions in Beijing made plain the ways that this policy undermines Chinese interests.

China enables Pyongyang's misbehavior. When dealing with North Korea, China walks softly and has discarded the stick.

Whether motivated by ties once as close as "lips and teeth," the desire to maintain whatever leverage China has in Pyongyang, or the fear that pressure might destabilize the North or prompt it to act out, Beijing refuses to crack down on North Korean misdeeds. Instead, it offers diplomatic cover and minimizes any punishment that might be agreed upon by the international community. For example, while Beijing quickly agreed to a UNSC [United Nations Security Council] Presidential Statement condemning the North's recent missile launch, it quickly whittled down the list of North Korean companies to be sanctioned from the 40 proposed by the US, EU [European Union], and others, to three. The result is a feeling of impunity in Pyongyang that leads to precisely the destabilizing behavior that Beijing says it fears. It has also bought China precious little goodwill in the North; Beijing is insistent on the need to give "face" to Pyongyang; with its antics, Pyongyang shows little regard for China's "face."

China antagonizes its neighbors. The readiness to back Pyongyang infuriates South Koreans. Beijing's fear of offending North Korea by even expressing condolences for the deaths of ROK [that is, the Republic of Korea, or South Korea] citizens after the sinking of the *Cheonan* [a South Korean navy ship sunk by a North Korean submarine in 2010, killing forty-six sailors] and the shelling of Yeonpyeong Island [a North Korea/South Korea military incident in 2010] has hardened South Korean feelings toward China. Nearly 92 percent of South Koreans were dissatisfied with Beijing's response to the shelling incident and more than 58 percent wanted Seoul to strongly protest, even if it meant damaging the economic relationship with China. More than 60 percent now consider China the biggest threat after reunification, almost three times as many as identified Japan. South Koreans are visibly offended by Beijing's call for "all parties" to act responsibly when it is North Korea that is the offender—and taking South Korean lives in the process. In informal trilateral discussions in Beijing last week [in May 2012], South Korean frustration was palpable. We have long heard similar views from Japanese.

Against Its Own Interests

China contributes to the strengthening of the US alliance system that it considers a tool of encirclement. Pyongyang's provocations, combined with China's refusal to do more to stop them, has driven Seoul and Tokyo to consolidate military relations with the US. Eager to strengthen the deterrent, US alliances in Northeast Asia are being modernized and reinforced, amid calls for enhancing US extended deterrence. Some in Seoul (and even more foolishly in the US Congress) are even calling for a redeployment of US tactical nuclear weapons to the Korean Peninsula. Their common concern regarding the North is such that South Korea and Japan are even stepping up bilateral coordination among themselves, a long-sought US goal, but one that has been hindered by historical animosity between Seoul and Tokyo.

China tarnishes its image as a supporter of international law and norms and undermines those norms. International law is hollow if it has "no teeth." The protection afforded Pyongyang and the refusal to see that UN sanctions have consequences undermines attempts to stop DPRK [that is, the Democratic People's Republic of Korea, or North Korea] misbehavior, encourages other governments to act in similar ways, and makes a mockery of international laws and institutions. Countries that would prefer to rely on international law instead develop ad hoc mechanisms to prevent illegal behavior. Beijing is seen as supporting international norms, principles, and laws that are ineffectual and have little impact on state behavior. China would be hard-pressed to more strongly signal support for an anarchic international system in which states are largely free to act as they please. Put more bluntly, the more Beijing—frequently aided and abetted by Moscow—renders the UN Security Council useless in dealing with the real challenges to international security, the more it encourages, if not necessitates, the creation of "coalitions of the willing" to deal with such problems.

China reinforces the US role in Northeast Asia and supports its international legitimacy. The reinforcement of US alliances more deeply embeds the US in the region. The growing role of those alliances signals their worth and value—and that of the US more generally—to other governments. The claims that China has marginal influence in North Korea and that the US is the real target of Pyongyang's activities highlights the significance, importance, and centrality of the US to regional diplomacy and affairs.

China blocks contingency planning that can keep a crisis from occurring or worsening. We are repeatedly warned that attempts to discuss North Korea in trilateral or multilateral settings would send the wrong signal to Pyongyang and spur it to act out. So, while experts concede that we need to prepare for a range of crises and contingencies, actually doing so isn't done for fear of antagonizing North Korea. In fact, such planning takes place without Beijing—this is part of the alliance strengthening. But China has interests in North Korea and is likely to intervene in the event of a crisis. Advanced discussions of how that might occur could minimize the risk that Chinese forces might reach a standoff—or worse—with allied forces in a crisis.

Change May Come

We could be snarky and say we're pleased that China is helping the US achieve its foreign policy objectives. But it is more accurate to say that we, like our South Korean and Japanese colleagues, are frustrated by the consequences of Beijing's self-defeating policies. North Korea continues to act out, endangering lives, risking the destabilization of Northeast Asia, and forcing other governments to divert resources that could be better used elsewhere. China is not the only country that seeks a stable Northeast Asia so that it can focus on economic development. Yet Beijing continues to pursue misguided, illogical and self-defeating policies.

There is some potential good news on the horizon, however. More and more frequently during our visits to China and during international conferences with Chinese scholars and even some officials, we witness our Chinese colleagues seriously debating one another over the logic behind Beijing's current policy. Many are truly embarrassed to be seen as Pyongyang's best (only?) friend and protector. They question whether you can actually have stability—China's primary objective—as long as the North has nuclear weapons. And, they acknowledge all the downsides highlighted above and an even more important one for the long term.

No one can predict when it will occur, but it is becoming increasingly clear that the peninsula will one day be reunited, under the political, economic, and social system that exists today in Seoul. The longer Beijing keeps the North on life support without insisting on the openness and reform that will set the stage for eventual peaceful reunification, the deeper will be the resentment of the Korean people and the greater will be their suspicion regarding China's long-term motives.

How this serves Beijing's interests remains beyond our ability to comprehend. At some point, one hopes that logic will finally prevail!

> *"While Western nations are seeking to dissuade North Korea from continuing with its nuclear program, the priority for the Chinese government is to maintain stability."*

North Korea: China Weighs Up Opposing North Korea Policies

Anny Boc

Anny Boc is a doctoral candidate, with interest in China's foreign and domestic politics, at the University of Cologne, as well as a contributor to Deutsche Welle. In the following viewpoint, she argues that traditionalist voices advocate continued support of the North Korean regime as a buffer state between China and US allies South Korea and Japan, while newer strategist voices advocate abandoning North Korea and increasing cooperation with the United States. However, a collapse of North Korea leading to reunification or a war provoked by North Korea could result in greater US military presence in the region, which is contrary to China's interest. Therefore, China, in general, maintains its existing policy but may begin to take a harder line toward North Korea, Boc concludes.

As you read, consider the following questions:

1. What event provoked Deng Yuwen, deputy editor of the *China's Study Times* journal, to call on China to "abandon North Korea"?

2. What group has traditionally had a significant influence on China's policy toward North Korea, according to the author?

3. What did US Defense Secretary Chuck Hagel recently announce, according to the author?

China has become more open than ever about its policy regarding North Korea. While some want a change of course as China seeks to keep instability from its door, others think the status quo should be preserved.

"North Korea's third nuclear test is a good moment for China to re-evaluate its long-standing alliance with the Kim dynasty," demanded Deng Yuwen, a guest columnist in the *Financial Times* newspaper. Deng, as deputy editor of the *China's Study Times* journal, published by the Beijing's Central Party School, called on China to "abandon North Korea."

Such comments represent a challenge to the decades-long friendship between the two Communist neighbors. Bilateral relations have reached a low point since the end of last year. Not only did North Korea provoke the world with its latest test in February this year, it also launched its Unha-3 rocket to successfully place a satellite in orbit around the earth.

Beijing, Pyongyang's only true ally, was openly annoyed with its unpredictable neighbor. Its patience had worn thin.

At the last general assembly of the National People's Congress, delegates took part in a debate about Chinese policy with regard to North Korea. The deputy director of the Central Foreign Affairs Office, Qiu Yuanping, reported that the debate ran as to whether China should continue to support its

China, North Korea, and the United States

The [Barack] Obama administration's public statements have emphasized common interests rather than differences in its policy toward China regarding North Korea. The United States also has been encouraging China to use its influence in Pyongyang to rein in the more provocative actions by North Korea. China's interests both overlap and coincide with those of the United States, but China's primary interest of stability on the Korean Peninsula is often at odds with U.S. interest in denuclearization and the provision of basic human rights for the North Korean people. Moreover, North Korean leaders appear to have used this interest to neutralize their country's growing economic dependence on China; the greater North Korea's dependency, the more fearful Chinese leaders may be that a sharp withdrawal of PRC [People's Republic of China] economic support could destabilize North Korea. Since the late 1990s, as long as North Korea has been able to convince Beijing's senior leadership that regime stability is synonymous with North Korea's overall stability, the Kim [Jong-il] government has been able to count on a minimum level of China's economic and diplomatic support.

Dick K. Nanto and Mark E. Manyin,
"China-North Korea Relations,"
Congressional Research Service, December 28, 2010.

neighbor or simply "drop" its alliance with Pyongyang. Her openness was unusual, the leadership in Beijing usually keeping tight-lipped on such matters.

Traditionalists vs. Strategists

Within Chinese political circles, opinion is split about how to deal with North Korea. Since the country conducted the second of its nuclear tests in 2009, two schools of thought have emerged.

The so-called traditionalists remain true to the image promoted by the founder of the People's Republic, Mao Zedong, that of a China and North Korea that was "as close as lips and teeth." For them, the idea that Beijing would ever abandon its Communist ally does not even arise. They see the United States as the greatest challenge to Chinese interests in East Asia. The strengthened military presence of the US in the Asia-Pacific region, a shift in strategic focus by US President Barack Obama's administration, is something that is widely perceived in Beijing to be a threat to national security. For China, North Korea represents something of a buffer state between it and South Korea and Japan, both strong US allies.

Until now, China's policy on North Korea has been significantly influenced by the People's Liberation Army. Given the long-standing ties with the country, and the mistrust of the US and its military power that prevails, the Chinese military leadership maintains the more conservative approach.

According to Jia Qingguo, professor of politics at Beijing University, this is an outdated strategy. China should use North Korea as a starting point to work more closely with the US, Jia—who would be described as one of the "strategists"—told the *New York Times*. The strategists advocate tougher measures by China against North Korea and, at the same time, increased cooperation with the US.

Security expert Zhang Liangui, of the Central Party School in Beijing, also calls for China to take a harder line with its neighbor. The belief that Pyongyang could be made to renounce nuclear weapons through a policy of appeasement is naïve, Zhang told the Chinese state newspaper *Global Times*.

No Major Change of Direction

"The support for tougher United Nations sanctions against North Korea should not be interpreted as a basic change in China's attitude," China's outgoing Foreign Minister Yang Jie-chi stressed. Yang is now responsible for foreign policy in the State Council of the People's Republic.

Experts believe that China possibly fears that the collapse of the regime in North Korea and a possible reunification of the two Koreas could see US troops deployed on the Chinese border. Paul Haenle, from the Carnegie Endowment for International Peace, who is also head of Beijing's Carnegie-Tsinghua Center, believes that the continuous provocation on the part of Pyongyang could, in the end, lead to an arms race.

"Like the US, both Japan and South Korea will also review their security strategy," said Haenle in an interview with DW. Such an outcome would be contrary to China's interests.

While Western nations are seeking to dissuade North Korea from continuing with its nuclear program, the priority for the Chinese government is to maintain stability, according to Stephanie Kleine-Ahlbrandt from the International Crisis Group.

"Beijing is worried about a direct military confrontation between Pyongyang and Washington," Kleine-Ahlbrandt told DW.

US Defense Secretary Chuck Hagel recently announced that Washington was bolstering its missile defense capabilities in response to threats by North Korea. Any war, or a collapse of the North Korean regime, would likely result in a flood of refugees from North Korea into northeastern China.

Under the leadership of China's new president Xi Jinping, however, it is unlikely there will be any radical changes, said Kleine-Ahlbrandt. "However, Beijing will adopt a harder line with North Korea."

"Given the South's manifold advantages over North Korea, an American military garrison is unnecessary. The troops should come home."

The United States Should Remove Its Troops from Korea

Doug Bandow

Doug Bandow is a senior fellow at the Cato Institute and the author of Tripwire: Korea and the US Foreign Policy in a Changed World. *In the following viewpoint, he argues that US policy in North Korea has failed. North Korea, he argues, has acquired nuclear weapons and is unlikely to give them up. Moreover, the United States has failed to enlist either South Korea or China in consistently pressuring the North. The status quo is unlikely to change. Therefore, Bandow concludes that the United States should pull its troops out of Korea and turn its attention elsewhere, leaving the countries of Northeast Asia to handle the region's problems.*

As you read, consider the following questions:

1. What evidence does Bandow point to which he says shows North Korea's unwillingness to give up its nuclear program?

Doug Bandow, "Pull U.S. Troops Out of Korea," Cato Institute, November 29, 2010. Reproduced by permission.

2. According to Bandow, why are South Korea's, Japan's, and China's policies toward North Korea unhelpful?

3. How does Bandow suggest that the United States could alter its nuclear policy in regard to Japan and South Korea?

Eight months after sinking a South Korean warship, North Korea launched an artillery barrage last week [in November 2010] against South Korean territory. Even worse, the North is a nuclear power.

North Korea's Nuclear Program

The U.S. should get used to it. Washington's drive to prevent the Democratic People's Republic of Korea [DPRK, that is, North Korea] from acquiring nuclear weapons is dead.

Yet the [Barack] Obama administration is pushing to restart nuclear negotiations with Pyongyang. Assistant Secretary of State Kurt Campbell recently opined: "We need to see a very clear signal that this new leadership—or some structure in North Korea—accepts the very clear commitments that North Korea made in 2005 to denuclearization."

There's little reason to believe those commitments were ever sincere. Nuclear weapons offer the Kim [Jong-il] regime obvious advantages internationally.

The domestic reasons are no less compelling. How better to run a "military first" policy than to give the armed services the ultimate weapon?

Whether Kim Jong-il was ever willing to trade away his nuclear program may never be known. Maybe he's still prepared to yield up future production. But he has given no indication that he is willing to turn over his existing arsenal.

Indeed, the regime appears to have restarted construction activity at the Yongbyon nuclear site, where in 2008 it demolished an old reactor's cooling tower. Moreover, the North Koreans last week unveiled a new uranium enrichment facility.

Pyongyang's recent policy towards the South has been unreservedly hostile. Last March the DPRK sank a South Korean corvette, the *Cheonan*, killing 46 sailors. Now, it has bombarded a South Korean island, killing four, including two civilians, and wounding a score of others.

Unfortunately, the situation is only likely to worsen as "Dear Leader" Kim Jong-il attempts to pass power on to his youngest son, Kim Jong-un. Despite the formal anointment at the recent meeting of the Korean Workers' Party, the succession may not be smooth.

There are many potential claimants for power—Kim Jong-il's sister and brother-in-law, a slightly older son criticized as effeminate by his father and an even older son by a different wife living in disgraced but luxurious exile in Macau. Plus numerous party and military officials who have been waiting for years for their turn at the top.

Moreover, an uncertain political environment discourages serious negotiation over nonproliferation. A weakened Dear Leader dependent on military support is not likely to sacrifice the nuclear weapons developed at enormous expense. No one struggling for power after his demise is likely to stand against the military.

Thus, the best outcome in the next several years likely is the status quo. Negotiations may not hurt, but they are unlikely to provide any discernible benefit.

Unfortunately, none of the DPRK's neighbors are inclined to be particularly helpful.

South Korea's policy has ranged from isolation of, to subsidies for, the North, while relying on the U.S. for its defense. Japan has subordinated policy towards the DPRK to resolving the status of Japanese citizens kidnapped by Pyongyang's agents in past years.

US Troop Reductions in Korea

Several aspects of the U.S.-R.O.K. [that is, the Republic of Korea, or South Korea] security relationship are changing as the U.S. moves from a leading to a supporting role. In 2004 an agreement was reached on the return of the Yongsan base in Seoul—as well as a number of other U.S. bases—to the R.O.K. and the eventual relocation of all U.S. forces to south of the Han River. Those movements are expected to be completed by 2016. In addition, the U.S. and R.O.K. agreed to reduce the number of U.S. troops in Korea to 25,000 by 2008, but a subsequent agreement by the U.S. and R.O.K. presidents in 2008 has now capped that number at 28,500, with no further troop reductions planned. The U.S. and R.O.K. have also agreed to transfer wartime operational control to the R.O.K. military on December 1, 2015.

US Department of State, "Background Notes:
South Korea," April 12, 2012.

The ever more assertive Beijing obviously believes that stability matters more than anything else. Indeed, the Chinese have been expanding investment in the North. The result has been to discourage reform.

Benign Neglect

Nothing is likely to change in the near future. Washington should step back and leave the issue to the North's neighbors.

The only Americans within easy reach of Pyongyang's weapons are the thousands of U.S. troops stationed in South Korea. Given the South's manifold advantages over North Korea, an American military garrison is unnecessary. The troops should come home.

Then Washington should adopt a policy of benign neglect towards the North. Let Seoul, Tokyo, and Beijing bear the risk of implosion, war, or proliferation.

In particular, the U.S. should point out to China that North Korea remains a potential national powder keg, with a rushed power transfer in the midst of a continuing economic crisis. Moreover, a regime willing to risk war with South Korea may make a deadlier miscalculation in the future.

Moreover, Washington should indicate that it does not intend to allow nonproliferation policy to leave only the bad guys with nuclear weapons. Should the North continue with its nuclear program, the U.S. would reconsider its opposition to the acquisition of nuclear weapons by South Korea and Japan.

Nuclear proliferation in Northeast Asia might be a nightmare, but if so, it will be one shared by Beijing.

Then the U.S. should turn its attention elsewhere.

Washington's policy towards the DPRK has failed. North Korea is a nuclear power and is unlikely to voluntarily surrender that status.

Rather than continue a fruitless campaign to denuclearize the North, the U.S. should hand off the problem to those nations with the most at stake in a peaceful and stable North Korea. Those nations with the most at stake should take the lead in resolving Northeast Asia's problems.

"*At this point, it would be difficult for the United States to withdraw from South Korea. The North Korean nuclear threat fixes the situation in place, even for troops that aren't relevant to that threat.*"

The United States Will Not Remove Its Troops from Korea

George Friedman

George Friedman is the founder and chief executive officer of the private intelligence corporation Stratfor and the coauthor of The Future of War: Power, Technology and American World Dominance in the Twenty-First Century. *In the following viewpoint, he argues that American troops are based in Korea largely because of inertia. He says that troops were left in the region following the Korean War and that they remain because all actors in the region—South Korea, Japan, China, and even North Korea—see them as a stabilizing presence. Friedman argues that the troops do not necessarily advance US geopolitical goals but moving them would require policy reconsiderations that no one in the region, nor the United States, wants to make.*

As you read, consider the following questions:

1. Why does Friedman say that the United States intervened in the Korean War?

2. According to Friedman, what is the North Korean survival strategy?

3. What does Friedman say has been the greatest achievement of the North Korean regime?

After U.S. president Barack Obama visited the Korean Demilitarized Zone on March 25 [2012] during his trip to South Korea for a nuclear security summit, he made the obligatory presidential remarks warning North Korea against continued provocations. He also praised the strength of U.S.-South Korean relations and commended the 28,500 U.S. troops stationed there. Obama's visit itself is of little importance, but it is an opportunity to ask just what Washington's strategy is in Korea and how the countries around North Korea (China, Russia, South Korea and Japan) view the region. As always, any understanding of current strategy requires a consideration of the history of that strategy.

The Korean War and the U.S. Proto-Strategy

Korea became a key part of U.S. Cold War–era containment strategy almost by accident. Washington, having deployed forces in China during World War II and thus aware of the demographic and geographic problems of operating on the Asian mainland, envisioned a maritime strategy based on the island chains running from the Aleutians to Java. The Americans would use the islands and the 7th Fleet to contain both the Soviets and the Chinese on the mainland.

Korea conceptually lay outside this framework. The peninsula was not regarded by the United States as central to its strategy even after the victory of the Communists in the Chinese civil war. After World War II, the Korean Peninsula, which had been occupied by the Japanese since the early 1900s, was divided into two zones. The North came under the control of Communists, the South under the control of a pro-American regime. Soviet troops withdrew from the North in 1948 and U.S. troops pulled out of the South the following year, despite some calls to keep them in place to dissuade Communist aggression. The actual U.S. policy toward an invasion of the South by the North is still being debated, but a U.S. intervention on the Korean Peninsula clearly violated Washington's core strategic principle of avoiding mainland operations and maintaining a strategic naval blockade.

U.S. strategy changed in 1950, when the North Koreans invaded the South, sparking the Korean War. Pyongyang's motives remain unclear, as do the roles of Moscow and Beijing in the decision. Obviously, Pyongyang wanted to unite the peninsula under Communist control, and obviously, it did not carry out its invasion against Chinese and Russian wishes, but it appears all involved estimated the operation was within the capabilities of the North Korean army. Had the North Korean military faced only South Korean forces, they would have been right. They clearly miscalculated the American intent to intervene, though it is not clear that even the Americans understood their intent prior to the intervention. However, once the North Koreans moved south, President Harry Truman decided to intervene. His reasoning had less to do with Korea than with the impact of a Communist military success on coalition partners elsewhere. The U.S. global strategy depended on Washington's ability to convince its partners that it would come to their aid if they were invaded. Strategic considerations aside, not intervening would have created a crisis of confidence, or so was the concern. Therefore, the United States intervened.

After serious difficulties, the United States managed to push the North Korean forces back into the North and pursue them almost to the Yalu River, which divides Korea and China. This forced a strategic decision on China. The Chinese were unclear on the American intent but did not underestimate American power. North Korea had represented a buffer between U.S. allies and northeastern China (and a similar buffer for the Soviets to protect their maritime territories). The Chinese intervened in the war, pushing the Americans back from the Yalu and suffering huge casualties in the process. The Americans regrouped, pushed back and a stalemate was achieved roughly along the former border and the current demilitarized zone. The truce was negotiated and the United States left forces in Korea, the successors of which President Obama addressed during his visit.

North Korea: The Weak, Fearsome Lunatic

The great mystery of the post–Cold War world is the survival of the North Korean regime. With a dynamic South, a non-Communist Russia and a China committed to good economic relations with the West, it would appear that the North Korean regime would have found it difficult to survive. This was compounded by severe economic problems (precipitated by the withdrawal of economic support from the Chinese and the Russians) and reported famines in the 1990s. But survive it did, and that survival is rooted in the geopolitics of the Cold War.

From the Chinese point of view, North Korea served the same function in the 1990s as it did in 1950: It was a buffer zone between the now economically powerful South Koreans (and the U.S. military) and Manchuria. The Russians were, as during the Korean War, interested in but not obsessed by the Korean situation, the more so as Russia shifted most of its attention west. The United States was concerned that a collapse in North Korea would trigger tensions with the Chinese and undermine the stability of its ally, South Korea. And the South Koreans were hesitant to undertake any actions that might trigger a response from North Korean artillery within range of Seoul, where a large portion of South Korea's population, government, industry and financial interests reside. In addition, they were concerned that a collapsing North would create a massive economic crisis in the South, having watched the difficulties of German integration [after communism collapsed in Eastern Europe in the late 1980s and East Germany and West Germany reunited in 1990] and recognizing the even wider economic and social gap between the two Koreas.

In a real sense, no one outside of North Korea was interested in changing the borders of the peninsula. The same calculations that had created the division in the first place and maintained it during and after the Korean War remained intact. Everyone either had a reason to want to maintain an independent North Korea (even with a Communist regime) or was not eager to risk a change in the status quo.

The most difficult question to answer is not how the United States viewed the potential destabilization of North Korea but rather its willingness to maintain a significant troop level in South Korea. The reason for intervening in the first place was murky. The U.S. military presence between 1953 and 1991 was intended to maintain the status quo during the Cold War. The willingness to remain beyond that is more complex.

Why Do Troops Remain?

Part of it simply had to do with inertia. Just as U.S. troops remain in Germany a generation after the end of the Cold War, it was easier not to reconsider U.S. strategy in Korea than to endure the internal stress of reconsidering it. Obviously, the United States did not want tensions between South Korea and North Korea, or to have the North Koreans misunderstand a withdrawal as an invitation to try another military move on the South, however unlikely. The Japanese saw Korean unification as problematic to their interests, since it could create a nearby industrial economic power of more than 70 million people and rekindle old rivalries. And North Korea, it would seem, actually welcomes the American presence, believing it limits South Korean adventurism. Between inertia and what we will call a proto-strategy, the United States remains.

With the loss of its Cold War patrons and the changing dynamic of the post–Cold War world, the North Koreans developed a survival strategy that Stratfor identified in the 1990s. The Koreans' intention was to appear—simultaneously—weak, fearsome and crazy. This was not an easy strategy to carry out, but they have carried it out well. First, they made certain that they were perceived to be always on the verge of internal collapse and thus not a direct threat to anyone but themselves. They went out of their way to emphasize their economic problems, particularly the famines in the 1990s. They wanted no one to think they were intent on being an aggressor unless provoked severely.

Second, they wanted to appear to be fearsome. This would at first blush seem to contradict the impression of weakness, but they managed it brilliantly by perpetually reminding the world that they were close to developing nuclear weapons and longer-range missiles. Recognizing that the Americans and Japanese had a reflexive obsession with nuclear weapons, Pyongyang constantly made it appear that they were capable of developing nuclear weapons but were not yet there. Not being there yet meant that no one had to do something about the weapons. Being close to developing them meant that it was dangerous to provoke them. Even North Korea's two nuclear tests have, intentionally or incidentally, appeared subpar, leaving its neighbors able to doubt the technological prowess of the "Hermit Kingdom."

The final piece was to appear crazy, or crazy enough that when pressed, they would choose the suicide option of striking with a nuclear weapon, if they had one. This was critical because a rational actor possessing one or a few weapons would not think of striking its neighbors, since the U.S. counterstrike would annihilate the North Korean regime. The threat wouldn't work if North Korea was considered rational, but, if it was irrational, the North Korean deterrence strategy could work. It would force everyone to be ultra-cautious in dealing with North Korea, lest North Korea do something quite mad. South Korean and U.S. propaganda did more for North Korea's image of unpredictability than the North could have hoped.

A Superb Strategy

North Korea, then, has spent more than two decades cultivating the image to the outside world of a nation on the verge of internal economic collapse (even while internally emphasizing its strength in the face of external threats). At the same time, the country has appeared to be on the verge of being a nuclear power—one ruled by potential lunatics. The net result was that the major powers, particularly South Korea, the United States and Japan, went out of their way to avoid provoking the North. In addition, these three powers were prepared to bribe North Korea to stop undertaking nuclear and missile development. Several times, they bribed the North with money or food to stop building weapons, and each time the North took the money and then resumed their program, quite ostentatiously, so as to cause maximum notice and restore the vision of the weak, fearsome lunatic.

The North was so good at playing this game that it maneuvered itself into a position in which it sat as an equal with the United States, Japan, Russia, China and South Korea—and it would frequently refuse to attend the Six-Party Talks. The ability to maneuver itself into a position equal to these powers was North Korea's greatest achievement, and it had a tremendous effect on stabilizing the regime by reinforcing its legitimacy internally and its power externally. Underneath this was the fact that no one was all that eager to see North Korea collapse, particularly since it was crazy and might have nuclear weapons. North Korea created a superb strategy for regime preservation in a very hostile region—or one that appeared hostile to the North Koreans.

Crucially for Pyongyang, North Korea was of tremendous use to one power: China. Even more than North Korea's role as a buffer state, its antics allowed China to emerge as mediator between the inscrutable Pyongyang and the frustrated United States. As China's economy grew, its political and military interests and reach expanded, leading to numerous tensions with the United States. But Beijing recognized that North Korea was a particular obsession of the United States because of its potential nuclear weapons and American sensitivity to weapons of mass destruction. Whenever North Korea did something outrageous, the United States would turn to China to address the problem. Having solved it, it was then inappropriate for Washington to press China on any other issue, at least for a while. Therefore, North Korea was a superb mechanism for the Chinese to deflect U.S. pressure on other issues.

For all of their occasional provocations, the North Koreans have been careful never to cross a line with conventional or nuclear power to compel a response from the South or the United States. Their ability to calibrate their provocations has been striking, even as their actions have escalated through nuclear tests to military action against South Korean ships and islands in the West Sea. Also striking is the manner in which those provocations have increased China's leverage with the United States.

The Difficulty of Extrication

At this point, it would be difficult for the United States to withdraw from South Korea. The North Korean nuclear threat fixes the situation in place, even for troops that aren't relevant to that threat. The troops could be withdrawn, but they won't be because the inertia of the situation makes it easier to leave them there than withdraw. As for the South Koreans, they simultaneously dislike the American presence and want it there, since it ensures U.S. military involvement in any crisis.

While the U.S. troop presence in Korea may not make the most sense in a global U.S. military strategy, it ironically seems to fit, at least for now, the interests of the Chinese, South Koreans and Japanese, and even in some sense the North Koreans. The United States, as the global power, therefore is locked into a deployment that does not match the regional requirements, requires endless explanation and is the source of frequent political complications. What we are left with is a U.S. strategy not based necessarily on the current situation but one tied to a historical legacy, left in place by inertia and held in place by the North Korean nuclear "threat."

Periodical and Internet Sources Bibliography

The following articles have been selected to supplement the diverse views presented in this chapter.

Agence France-Presse	"South Korea, US Practise Occupying North Korea in Military Drill," *Australian*, September 11, 2012.
Jayshree Bajoria and Beina Xu	"The China-North Korea Relationship," Council on Foreign Relations, February 21, 2012.
Jayshree Bajoria and Youkyung Lee	"The U.S.-South Korea Alliance," Council on Foreign Relations, October 13, 2011.
Ralph A. Cossa	"Japan-South Korea Relations: Time to Open Both Eyes," Council on Foreign Relations, July 2012.
Economist	"South Korea's Pop-Cultural Exports: Hallyu, Yeah!," January 25, 2010.
Ben Hancock	"US Forces OK in ROK—For Now," *Diplomat*, March 2, 2010.
Steve Herman	"Japan, S. Korea Disputed Island Spat Heats Up," VOA News, August 21, 2012.
Stephanie Kleine-Ahlbrandt	"The Dimishing Returns of China's North Korea Policy," 38 North, August 16, 2012.
Foster Klug and Youkyung Lee	"'Gangam Style' Rides Viral Wave to 220 Mil. Views," *China Post*, September 24, 2012.
Louisa Lim	"South Korean Culture Wave Spreads Across Asia," NPR, March 26, 2006.
Evan Ramstad	"Movement in the China-NK Relationship?," *Wall Street Journal*, April 19, 2012.
Yun Sun	"The Logic of China's Korea Policy," *Diplomat*, June 22, 2012.

OPPOSING
VIEWPOINTS®
SERIES

CHAPTER 3

Does North Korea Present a Serious Threat to the World?

Chapter Preface

North Korea has invested heavily in weapons of mass destruction. This includes the development of dangerous chemical and biological weapons capabilities.

In a June 18, 2009, report, the International Crisis Group said that there is no exact estimate of the extent of North Korea's chemical weapons program. However, it is estimated that the country has 2500–5000 tons of chemical agents, including mustard gas, phosgene gas, and sarin gas, among other weapons. Though the report says that the North is not actively increasing its capabilities, it notes that the stockpile available is already "sufficient to inflict massive civilian casualties on South Korea." The North also has multiple technologies to deliver chemical weapons, including long-range artillery, rocket launchers, ballistic missiles, and aircraft.

In addition to the threat to South Korea, North Korea's stockpile is worrisome because the North might be tempted to sell chemical agents or knowledge about creating and delivering chemical agents to other countries or terrorist groups.

North Korea's biological weapons program is much more shadowy than its chemical weapons one. South Korea believes that North Korea has produced anthrax, botulinum toxin, and smallpox for potential military use. But verification is difficult, in part because legitimate biological research facilities can be easily converted to the creation of biological weapons, according to J. Berkshire Miller in a November 12, 2011, article in the *Diplomat*. Miller adds that confronting North Korea's biological weapons program has been hampered by weaknesses in the international regulatory system. North Korea has signed the Biological Weapons Convention—officially known as the Convention on the Prohibition of the Development, Production and Stockpiling of Bacteriological (Biological) and Toxin Weapons and on Their Destruction—but since the convention does not have strong enforcement or inspection provisions, it has largely served to conceal North Korea's weapons program rather than to regulate it. To make matters worse, while South Korea has strong defense capabilities against a chemical attack, it has only begun to invest in defenses against biological weapons.

North Korea has never used chemical and biological weapons against another nation. However, there are reports that it has tested these agents on its own political prisoners. One former political prisoner, Soon Ok Lee, was quoted by Simon Cooper in an October 1, 2009, essay in *Popular Mechanics*. Lee said she witnessed one test and described the aftermath. "I saw many prisoners lying on the slope of a hill, bleeding from their mouths and motionless, enveloped by strange fumes and surrounded by scores of guards in the gas masks . . . I delivered earlier in the morning."

As alarming as North Korea's biological and chemical weapons capabilities are, its nuclear program continues to be the focus of most world attention. This chapter examines controversies surrounding the danger posed by North Korea's nuclear ambitions.

"It is important to prepare for a window of opportunity to reengage [North Korea] on the nuclear issue under its new, untried leadership in early 2013."

A Leadership Transition May Reduce the North Korean Threat

Peter Hayes, Scott Bruce, and David von Hippel

Peter Hayes is adjunct professor of international relations at the Royal Melbourne Institute of Technology and director of the Nautilus Institute for Security and Sustainability; Scott Bruce is an associate at the Nautilus Institute and the East-West Center; David von Hippel is a senior associate at the Nautilus Institute. In the following viewpoint, they argue that the death of North Korean leader Kim Jong-il and the transition of power to his son Kim Jong-un may provide an opportunity for lowered tensions and progress. The authors argue that a new generation of Korean leaders are more aware of, and interested in engaging with, the outside world. If Kim Jong-un can consolidate power quickly, and if, as his background suggests, he is less insular than his father, the authors conclude that change may come to North Korea.

As you read, consider the following questions:

1. How did Kim Jong-il promote the power of his clan before his death, according to the authors?

2. What shift in leadership style do the authors say occurred in North Korea after power passed away from Kim Il-sung?

3. What do the authors cite as a stunning example of the leading edge of the structural change in North Korea?

When North Korean leader and founding father Kim Il-sung died in July 1994, his son Kim Jong-il had held the reins of power since he was anointed in 1981—for 15 years. Kim Jong-il only took over fully in 1994 because his father dropped dead, having just reached over his shoulder to take back the reins in order to meet with President Jimmy Carter, to make a deal that averted a head-on collision with the United States over the North's nuclear program at Yongbyon. The problem with Kim Jong-il dying during an "on the spot guidance" on December 17 [2011]—as announced today by the North Korean official media on December 19 at 1830—is that not much is known about his third son and designated 27-year-old successor, Kim Jong-un. Indeed, he has only ever appeared in public accompanied by his father after nearly 14 months in the limelight. Moreover, he has had only one year, not 15, to prepare for leadership, although his grooming clearly began in 2008. His rise to power is far more abrupt than his father who was withdrawn from public view for 3 years after 1981.

Kim Jong-un

Kim Jong-un is said to have studied in Switzerland, he reportedly speaks English and German, and spent time training in the artillery command of the Korean People's Army before his rapid ascension to four-star general and membership of the

Central Military Commission—the voice of leadership when it comes to setting the party and military line on critical issues at key junctures, especially in confrontations with external powers.

Before he died, Kim Jong-il had also strengthened the courtly power of his clan, by promoting his sister and her husband to create, with Kim Jong-un, a triumvirate with which to continue the dynastic succession.

Kim Jong-un's skills as a decisive leader, his charismatic ability to mobilize and motivate people, and his skill at manipulating the many levers of power and control in the DPRK's [the Democratic People's Republic of Korea's, or North Korea's] pyramid of power, however, all remain untested, at least insofar as those outside the DPRK, can determine.

Kim Jong-un did not accompany Kim Jong-il in his May 2011 visit to China, now the DPRK's main geopolitical and economic backer, although he did meet him at the border upon return, thereby linking his stature to that of his father. Kim Jong-un did, however, meet with a high level PLA [Chinese army] delegation in Pyongyang on October 25, 2010, led by Colonel General Guo Boxiong, PRC [People's Republic of China] Central Military [Commission] vice chairman. At that time, Guo gave to him a framed calligraphy that read in Chinese: "In the Same Strain"—an obvious reference to Kim Il-sung and a blessing from the Chinese military of his succession.

This emblem of support from the military, plus the observation of China's heavy economic investment in recent years in the physical infrastructure of North Korea in order to extract resources (chiefly coal, iron ore, and other minerals) at relatively low prices from the DPRK, suggests that China will continue to back the Kim regime under Kim Jong-un. China's decisive strategic support after the two major confrontations between the DPRK and South Korea—in March when the ROK [the Republic of Korea, or South Korea] warship *Cheo-*

nan was sunk, almost certainly by the North; and November, when the North shelled Yeonpyeong Island and killed not only soldiers, but civilians for the first time since the Korean Armistice stilled the guns in 1953—is another indicator that China's support is likely to persist.

Now, in addition to the national celebrations of the 100th year of Kim Il-sung's birthday in 2012, the new leader must steer the DPRK through a long period of mourning for Kim Jong-il, while focusing on improving the domestic economy.

A New Leadership Style?

Here, the generational factor may make a major difference to the style of decision making and the relative decentralization of power in the DPRK. Already, political scientists have noted that North Korea shifted from one-man, totalitarian leadership in the person of Kim Il-sung to a more technocratic style called authoritarian pluralism under Kim Jong-il, where he let the agencies of state—basically the military, the cabinet representing the economic line agencies, and the foreign affairs ministry—articulate different policy options—and then he would make a decisive move that set the cast.

Nowhere was this more evident than on the nuclear issue when, at the most tense moments, the pronouncements and results of decisions by the National Defense Commission would boom forth in ways that settled debates and set the line to follow.

However, the gerontocrats who lived through the Korea War are almost all gone; the next generation of senior leaders—the forty-five to sixty-year-old North Koreans in senior party, military, and economic positions of power—are remarkably well educated and often well informed about the DPRK's relative and absolute backwardness. These people are connected by family, school, and university networks. They number perhaps 5,000 key people in leadership positions, and overall, perhaps 100,000 including dependent kin. They watch

The Shadowy Figure of Kim Jong-un

North Korean dictator Kim Jong-il reportedly suffered a stroke in August of 2008, giving the question of who would succeed him new importance and urgency. The country's government stemmed from a hybrid of hereditary dynasty and communism through which power had passed exclusively from father to son since 1945, so it was only natural to look to Kim Jong-il's three sons to discover the next ruler. The eldest, Kim Jong-nam, was once considered the favorite, but apparently fell into disfavor after being caught trying to sneak into Japan under a fake passport in 2001. The second son, Kim Jong-chol, did not appear to have ever been seriously considered as the heir. And thus the youngest, Kim Jong-un, became widely viewed as his father's [successor].

The veil of secrecy and falsification that had long enveloped the country's rulers seemed to have been drawn especially tightly around the youngest son. . . .

Despite the dearth of facts, however, analysts generally agreed that Kim Jong-un was born on January 8, 1983 (others suggest 1984). . . . Although many believed he attended the International School of Berne, later reports surmised that he had attended Switzerland's more modest Liebefeld-Steinhölzli School. . . . He reportedly left there in 2000 and went on to attend the Kim Il-sung Military University back in North Korea. Career details were equally sketchy, but Kim Jong-un was purported to be working in either the prominent Organization Guidance Department of the Korean Workers' Party or the army's influential General Political Bureau in 2007. By 2009 there were rumors that he had been put in unofficial charge of the country's extremely powerful National Defense Commission and been assigned the title "Brilliant Comrade."

"Kim Jong-un," Biography in Context. *Detroit: Gale, 2009.*

each other's backs, and enjoy a privileged, albeit spartan lifestyle, compared to their hungry compatriots.

Many of them are well traveled and even cosmopolitan, not unlike their South Korean counterparts, and understand the need for massive and structural change to their economy and polity. However, they also understand that too rapid a change could lead to chaos and disaster, so they are cautious and know what a weak hand they have to play, both against the politically conservative and socially influential military, and against the South and its many allies, especially the United States.

As a stunning example of the leading edge of this structural change, today more than 800,000 North Koreans have cell phones—grown from a few tens of thousands in just two or three years, and far more than can be monitored individually and centrally, as was the practice in the good old days of totalitarian surveillance of all telecommunications. In the midst of its deprivation, the DPRK was in this respect, at least, busy building the foundations of a middle class, and sought to use its nuclear weapons as a way to compel external powers to assist it economically. Kim Jong-un is likely even more conversant than this new generation of senior leaders with the Internet and networked information economies, and therefore, likely to be more open to rapid, structural change in the economy. Whether he can bring along his senior advisors in embracing the notion of structural change is another matter—but for once, time is on his side, and he can press for change knowing that domestic and international forces will likely support him in the search for resolution of the nuclear issue.

Continuity and Possible Change

Initially, Kim Jong-un and his senior advisors are likely to seek continuity with the past as the basis for smooth sailing in 2012 while they concentrate on domestic issues. Thus, they will emphasize their relationships with China; they will continue to talk about reengaging in the Six-Party Talks [with South Korea, the United States, China, Russia, and Japan] on the nuclear issue, but are unlikely to actually participate given the need for clear policy lines to be articulated at the talks; and they will avoid provocations at the DMZ [demilitarized zone between North and South Korea] in 2012 to channel the political and emotional mobilization associated with the mourning of Kim Jong-il's passing to merge into support for Kim Jong-un's leadership.

Ironically, Kim Jong-il's death may make Korea the land of the morning calm for at least a year, during which political transitions will also occur in China, South Korea, Japan, Russia, and the United States. Far from a "Korean Spring" led by 27-year-old revolutionaries, while the process of domestic change has begun in the DPRK at the very top and may prove to be just as irresistible as in the Arab world, the transition is likely to start quietly.

Of course, it is possible to envision bleaker outcomes. One is a struggle within the Kim clique. Another is division within the center and provincial military leaderships if the 3rd Kim coming to power results in paralysis of central decision making. Chaos in mid-winter could result in a major humanitarian crisis. The military might object to diplomatic moves to trade away nuclear weapons in return for little more than some fuel and surplus corn from America.

In part to avoid these possibilities, but also to exploit the new space that Kim Jong-un may open up, it is important to prepare for a window of opportunity to reengage the DPRK on the nuclear issue under its new, untried leadership in early 2013. Unless Kim Jong-un throws the nuclear strategy out the window and starts again, the outlines of this engagement agenda are already clear—send the North Koreans energy and food aid to meet both short-term humanitarian and medium/long-term development needs, help them build a safe small light water reactor, and bring them into an international enrichment consortium that would lead them to reveal the sum total of their enrichment program.

| *"Foolish politicians around the world, including the puppet forces in South Korea, . . . should not expect any changes."*

The Leadership Transition Shows Little Sign of Reducing the North Korean Threat

Justin McCurry

Justin McCurry is the Guardian's *Tokyo correspondent. In the following viewpoint, he reports that after Kim Jong-un took power, North Korea issued aggressive statements insisting that there would be no change in policy toward the South. McCurry says that this is a disappointment, since some commenters had hoped that the North might move toward a less aggressive policy following the change in leadership. While some still hold out hope that the North will become less aggressive, North Korea's rhetoric has diminished the possibility for a quick movement toward reconciliation or a drawdown of North Korea's nuclear program, according to McCurry.*

As you read, consider the following questions:

1. According to McCurry, what South Korean policy decision did North Korea most strongly condemn?

2. What progress does a US expert say that North Korea has made toward nuclear capabilities?

3. What caused ties between North Korea and South Korea to deteriorate in 2010, according to McCurry?

Hopes for a new era of engagement with North Korea have faded after the country's powerful defence commission warned the world not to expect a change in policy under its new leader, Kim Jong-un.

Sea of Fire

The announcement broadcast by the state-run Korean Central News Agency on Friday [in December 2011], effectively dashed hopes that Kim might be ready to engage with South Korea and the wider international community.

In comments attributed to the national defence commission, the agency said "foolish politicians" should expect no change in policy and threatened South Korea's conservative president, Lee Myung-bak, with a "sea of fire".

"We declare solemnly and confidently that foolish politicians around the world, including the puppet forces in South Korea, that they should not expect any changes from us," the commission said.

It reserved its strongest criticism for Lee's refusal to allow ordinary South Koreans to pay their respects to the former North Korean leader Kim Jong-il, who died a fortnight ago. Only a former first lady and the chairwoman of the Hyundai group, whose husbands had strong ties to the North, were permitted to travel to Pyongyang to view Kim's body.

Lee, who has ditched the "sunshine policy" of engagement pioneered by Kim Dae-jung in the late 1990s, ended unconditional aid to the North in 2008. Pyongyang, the commission said, would "refuse forever to engage with traitor Lee Myung-bak and his group".

It added: "The world shall clearly see how the millions of our soldiers and people, who united firmly round great leader comrade Kim Jong-un to transform sorrow into courage and tears into strength, will achieve the final victory.

"The sea of bloody tears from our military and people will follow the puppet regime until the end. The tears will turn into a sea of revengeful fire that burns everything."

Limited Hopes

Koh Yu-hwan, a North Korea expert at Dongguk University in Seoul, said the statement did not necessarily mean that Pyongyang was averse to reform.

"It is raising the stakes in case the South wants better relations so Pyongyang can extract greater concessions," Koh told the Associated Press, adding that it was "too early to say the North is dashing hopes for reforms".

The North frequently issues statements heavy with bellicose rhetoric, but the commission's statement, coming a day after the country named Kim Jong-un its "Supreme Leader," bodes ill for the prospects of multiparty talks on North Korea's nuclear weapons programme.

The North is known to have the material needed to build nuclear weapons. Earlier this week a US expert said he believed the regime was one or two years away from mounting a warhead on a medium-range missile.

The US will attempt to calm fears of regional instability when the assistant secretary of state for East Asian and Pacific affairs, Kurt Campbell, travels to Beijing, Seoul and Tokyo early next month to discuss the global response to the new regime.

The US and South Korean defence chiefs on Thursday reiterated their commitment to stability on the Korean Peninsula.

The Pentagon said that the two countries "shared the view that peace and stability on the Korean Peninsula is our overarching priority and agreed to maintain close cooperation and coordination in the weeks and months ahead".

Cross-border ties deteriorated dramatically last year after the North shelled Yeonpyeong Island, a South Korean territory close to the countries' maritime border in the Yellow Sea. North Korea has also been blamed for the 2010 torpedo attack on the *Cheonan*, a South Korean naval vessel, in which 46 sailors died.

North and South Korea signed a truce, but not a peace treaty after their 1950–53 conflict and remain technically at war, separated by a heavily fortified border.

"North Korea has not only developed nuclear weapons, [but] it is also building missiles that could, in [the] future, reach Australia."

North Korea Is a Serious Nuclear Threat to Australia and the World

Kevin Rudd

Kevin Rudd is an Australian politician who has served as both minister of foreign affairs and prime minister. In the following viewpoint, he argues that North Korea's nuclear threat poses a serious danger to Australia. He says that North Korea is well on its way to developing nuclear bombs and is also developing missiles that could carry those bombs all the way to Australia. He adds that North Korea is unpredictable and aggressive. He concludes that Australia should continue to work to isolate North Korea, to advance nuclear nonproliferation, and to ally itself closely with the military might of the United States.

As you read, consider the following questions:

1. How many nuclear bombs does Rudd say North Korea could make, and what tests has the regime conducted?

2. What missiles does Rudd say North Korea is developing that could threaten Australia?

3. According to Rudd, what steps has Australia taken to promote a nuclear weapons–free world?

It is now twenty years since the end of the Cold War [political and military tension between the United States and the Soviet Union that ended in 1991]. So Australia should be safe from nuclear attack, right?

Think again.

Targeting Australia

In the far north of our region, the secretive North Koreans are hard at work to threaten our allies, our region and us. North Korea has not only developed nuclear weapons, [but] it is also building missiles that could, in [the] future, reach Australia: Darwin, Brisbane or even Sydney.

Too scary?

Let's look at the facts.

Experts estimate that North Korea has enough material to make up to eight nuclear bombs, right now.

They are busy making sure that their bombs will work. They have so far conducted two nuclear tests, in 2006 and 2009. These tests have not necessarily gone entirely to plan but they are making progress and determined to succeed.

At the same time, they are finding new ways to make the ingredients for nuclear weapons. In defiance of its previous agreements and UN [United Nations] sanctions, they have resumed work to produce more plutonium. Worse, they have unveiled a brand-new uranium enrichment plant, a technically more advanced way of producing larger amounts of nuclear material and, in turn, more bombs.

What makes this especially worrying is that they are also planning to create the most lethal cocktail there is: a nuclear warhead mounted on a missile.

North Korea is believed to have more than 800 ballistic missiles, with a range of up to 3000km [kilometers]. This is deeply worrying for our close friends in the region.

But we in Australia have no cause for comfort.

North Korea is developing new missiles, with a much longer range. The Taepodong-2 could travel as far as 9000km, bringing it within reach of northern Australia as well as the United States. Darwin is less than 6000km from North Korea. Sydney is about 8500km.

While tests of this missile in 2006 and 2009 were only partially successful, North Korea has left no one in any doubt about its determination to eventually field intercontinental ballistic missiles and to miniaturise nuclear bombs so that their missiles can carry them, as difficult a challenge as this is.

Some might ask why North Korea would risk a war with its neighbours and the US. Well, let's consider just how dangerous North Korea's behaviour has been in recent years. Since announcing its withdrawal from the Nuclear Non-Proliferation Treaty [officially known as the Treaty on the Non-Proliferation of Nuclear Weapons] in 2003, North Korea has not just tested nuclear bombs and missiles. It has conducted artillery attacks against South Korea and sunk one of its naval vessels, resulting in the death of 50 people.

Dangerous and Unpredictable

Let's be clear. The regime in Pyongyang is dangerous. Its behaviour is often unpredictable. But one thing about it we can predict is it being hell-bent on building a nuclear arsenal.

We should not be lulled into a false sense of security by the dire state of the country's economy. In fact, North Korea's weapons programs are a source of funding for the regime. It sells its weapons secrets for hard currency that keeps the regime's coffers stocked. Countries like Syria and Iran are buyers.

"What's on Your Mind?," cartoon by Ed Fischer, www.CartoonStock.com. Copyright ©
by Ed Fischer. Reproduction rights obtainable from www.CartoonStock.com. All rights
reserved. Reproduced by permission.

Make no mistake, the North Korean regime is armed and
dangerous. It has a long history of brinkmanship and has
shown that it is prepared to lash out. A cruel totalitarian state,
it has no regard for the welfare of its people, much less world
opinion.

North Korea's generals are, of course, under no illusion
that their forces can match the US and its allies in strategic
terms. Their plan is not to win any fight, but to threaten so
much damage that adversaries will not challenge them.

That is why we must work with our friends and partners
to stare down North Korea's provocations. We need to tighten
sanctions against its leadership and counter its weapons programs in every practical way that we can.

That's one reason why our recent alliance talks with the
Americans were so important. A key advantage that we have

in countering threats to our security is our deep partnership with the United States—still the most powerful military nation on earth by a country mile.

The North Korean threat is also a reason why Australia has placed itself at the forefront of efforts for a nuclear weapons–free world. At the UN last week [in September 2011], we pushed to bring a nuclear test ban treaty into force. We worked to strengthen the Nuclear Non-Proliferation Treaty. And we worked to strengthen security cooperation in our region. We also need China, with its special links to the regime, to bring the North Koreans under control.

North Korea is not an abstract threat. It is real. It is worsening. And it could prove to be our worst nightmare.

| *"The situation isn't urgent."*

North Korea Is Not a Serious Nuclear Threat to the United States

Fred Kaplan

Fred Kaplan is a journalist who writes the column War Stories for Slate. In the following viewpoint, he argues that North Korea is not a serious threat to the United States. He points out that North Korea missile tests have been failures, that its nuclear bomb tests have been unimpressive, and that it is therefore not a nuclear threat to America. He suggests, therefore, that the United States should assure North Korea that any provocation will be met firmly and should then ignore the regime as much as possible.

As you read, consider the following questions:

1. What tactical error does Kaplan say the Obama administration made in its February 29, 2012, accord with North Korea?

2. What is a major obstacle to US efforts to ignore North Korea, according to Kaplan?

3. Why does Kaplan contend China cannot force North
   Korea to behave?

The North Koreans can be such a pain, so wearying, you
wish that you could just ignore them. So let's do that.
Let's ignore them. For the moment, it might be, strategically,
the best thing we can do.

Failed Launch

Their latest escapade, which some analysts have since hyped as
a threat and harbinger of crisis, was the attempt on April 13
[2012] to launch a missile into space. (Pyongyang's foreign
ministry insisted that the payload was merely a peaceful satellite, but this was a ruse and, in any case, irrelevant: A rocket
that can spin a satellite into orbit can also release a nuclear
warhead.)

The launch, of course, was a dreadful, stupid thing. On
Feb. 29, the [President Barack] Obama administration had
signed an accord with the North Koreans, agreeing to provide
them with 240,000 tons of food aid over the next year if they
suspended all missile and nuclear tests—and here they were,
violating the deal just six weeks later, which suggested that
they'd been planning the launch while signing on the dotted
line.

But the headline is this: The missile sputtered and shat-
tered into a million pieces a few seconds after blast off—the
same ending that's marked all their long-range missile tests.

In response, Obama cut off the food aid and pushed a
resolution through the U.N. [United Nations] Security Council denouncing the launch as a "serious violation" of international law. That was the proper response (though it was a tactical mistake for Obama to link food aid with an arms accord
in the first place—food should be given as humanitarian assistance, not foisted as a political bargaining chip; a link to energy supplies would have been more fitting).

Walk Away

Now what should we do? Shrug, and say "Well, we tried to give Li'l Kim [that is, Kim Jong-un, the new leader of North Korea] a chance," and walk away.

Two days after the failed launch, as if to tack a sicko punch line to a lame joke, Kim Jong-un, the Hermit Kingdom's new 28-year-old pygmy tyrant, delivered a public speech boasting of North Korea's "military superiority" and vowing not to succumb to imperialist pressure.

This was typical rhetoric from the Kim dynasty—[Kim] Il-sung, [Kim] Jong-il, and now Jong-un, who often come off as the Borats [referring to a fictional character portrayed by comedian Sacha Baron Cohen and presented as a clueless foreigner] of international communism. What should we do about that speech and others like it? Nothing, except maybe giggle.

Are the North Koreans a threat? Not to the United States, not remotely. They have enough plutonium to build at most a handful of nuclear weapons, though whether they've built them, nobody knows. They've conducted underground tests twice, one in 2006, the other in 2009. The explosive power in both instances ranked extremely slight in the annals of nuclear coming-out parties.

There are signs that they're preparing to test a uranium bomb. (The others were plutonium.) If they do, and if it's a little bit more awesome than the earlier tests, the proper response, again, is . . . well, not quite to ignore it, but almost.

One obstacle to silence on this score is that we have allies in the region. Specifically, South Korea and Japan can't be expected to strike a cool pose in the shadow of Pyongyang's bomb. Nor can the United States, their ultimate guarantor of security, sit back and whistle as if nothing had happened. Doing so might send a signal, to all concerned, that we *accept* North Korea's status as a nuclear power.

So, yes, the Obama administration should, again, issue the obligatory condemnation, draft a resolution for the U.N. Security Council, and ratchet up sanctions against Pyongyang's *regime*. Just don't expect this to result in much.

But more to the point, don't get bent out of shape. That would only play into their game. The North Korean leaders savor our attention. They grow a little in their own delusional stature every time we shudder over the grave danger they allegedly pose. They shine a little brighter in the domestic propaganda that touts them, and justifies their totalitarian rule, as the much-feared protectors of the Great Korean Nation.

Scott Snyder, in his seminal book *Negotiating on the Edge*, describes North Korea's diplomatic style as "a prolonged cycle of crisis, intimidation and brinksmanship." The trick to countering it is to break the cycle, and one way to do that is not to get sucked into it.

A Shrimp Among Whales

Instead of exaggerating their strength, we should solidify our own. Snyder notes the shrewd strategy pioneered by Kim Il-sung (North Korea's founder and the current Kim's grandfather) of behaving like a "shrimp among whales," maximizing his leverage by playing the whales—the much larger, often hostile nations all around him—off one another.

The best way to counter that strategy is to disarm it. Clasp close to South Korea and Japan. Appear, smiling, with their leaders at every opportunity. Sign accords of all sort, meaningful or otherwise. Hold the occasional joint military exercise. Let loose a head-spinning statistic now and then, on how much air, sea, and ground power we could amass on the Korean Peninsula while barely lifting a finger. Don't brandish any of this. Do it all casually. Float like a butterfly, and quietly, calmly, let the North Koreans know how painful our bee sting will be if they pull anything like the crazy mischief they often threaten to unleash.

North Korea's Nuclear History

In 2002, the United States announced that North Korea admitted that it had a secret weapons program. North Korea asserted its right to weapons development, started the removal of the IAEA [International Atomic Energy Agency] surveillance equipment from its facilities and expelled two IAEA inspectors. In 2003, United States officials stated that North Korea claimed to have completed the reprocessing of 8000 spent fuel rods at what it called its nuclear deterrent facility at Yongbyon. North Korea stated publicly that it would build a nuclear deterrent 'unless the United States gives up its hostile policy.' On August 27, 2003, the Six-Party Talks opened between North Korea, on the one hand, and the United States, Japan, China, Russia and South Korea, on the other. In December 2003, North Korea declared its willingness to freeze its nuclear program in return for a list of concessions by the United States. By the end of 2005, however, nothing much was accomplished. . . .

Between July 4th and 5th, 2006, North Korea test fired seven missiles as a result of which the [United Nations] Security Council voted to impose sanctions on the state. The resolution instructed states to ban the exports of missile-related material to North Korea and instructed North Korea to halt its ballistic missile program. . . . On October 6, 2006, North Korea claimed that it had tested a nuclear weapon in a safe and successful manner and called this a historic event. A few days later, the United States announced that air samples collected from the test site confirmed that North Korea had carried out an underground nuclear explosion of less than 1 kiloton.

Elli Louka, Nuclear Weapons, Justice and the Law. Cheltenham, UK: Edward Elgar, 2011, pp. 148–149.

If a deal of some sort seems worthwhile and feasible, obviously, we should explore it. If not, we should pay more attention to important matters that we might affect.

There was a time when Pyongyang could be dealt with. In fact, President Bill Clinton did deal with it. The agreed framework, signed in 1994, halted North Korea's plutonium program—and installed permanent inspectors in its reprocessing plant—for eight years. (Scott Snyder's book is basically a guide to North Korea's negotiating style and how to engage it.) In the opening weeks of George W. Bush's presidency, Secretary of State Colin Powell told reporters that he'd pick up where Clinton left off. Bush came down on Powell hard. To Bush and [vice president] Dick Cheney, you didn't negotiate with evil; you defeated it. Pyongyang tried to reengage through various intermediaries, to no avail. So the North Koreans restarted their nuclear program, built a bomb, and tested it—at which point Bush offered to go back to the negotiating table, ill-prepared and too late.

Bush's fallacy was thinking that the North Korean regime would collapse under the slightest pressure. The regime proved more durable—and Kim Jong-il, the "dear leader" of the time, much shrewder—than he or Cheney had imagined.

Obama's fallacy is thinking that China can be prodded to force Kim & Co. to behave. That isn't likely to happen, either. The Chinese leaders seem annoyed when North Korea launches a missile or sets off a bomb. But their primary interest in that part of the world is stability. They want above all to avert a collapse of Pyongyang's regime, which might set off a humanitarian crisis of massive proportions as millions—perhaps tens of millions—of North Koreans cross the border to flee the ensuing chaos, exploit the sudden liberation, or both. China's secondary interest in the region is to keep American air and naval forces bottled up in Northeast Asia and thus minimize the strength they can mobilize around the Taiwan straits. In other words, unless Kim Jong-un does something way more outlandish than anything his forefathers attempted, China is not interested in putting much pressure on North Korea to change its ways.

Daniel Sneider, associate director of the [Walter H.] Shorenstein Asia-Pacific Research Center at Stanford University, advises a course of "strategic patience" when it comes to North Korea. "Deterrence, containment, engagement when it's possible and productive—we shouldn't have any problem doing that," he says. "The situation isn't urgent."

> *"U.S. interest in re-engaging with North Korea is also driven by concern that, in the absence of a negotiating process, there is no practical way to restrain North Korea from expanding its nuclear and missile programs."*

Talks with the United States Could Reduce the North Korean Nuclear Threat

Evans J.R. Revere

Evans J.R. Revere is a nonresident senior fellow with the Center for Northeast Asian Policy Studies at the Brookings Institution, and he served as deputy head of the US negotiating team with North Korea from 1998–2000. In the following viewpoint, he argues that dialogue with North Korea is important for a number of reasons. First, he says, it helps the United States anticipate North Korea's actions; second, it helps the United States convey its position to North Korea; and finally, it helps manage crises. Revere says dialogue may also help control some aspects of North Korea's nuclear program, but he cautions against the belief that the talks can completely halt North Korea's nuclear efforts.

Evans J.R. Revere, *Re-Engaging North Korea After Kim Jong-il's Death: Last, Best Hope or Dialogue to Nowhere?*, The Brookings Institution, Policy Paper, no. 29, January 2012. Copyright © 2012 The Brookings Institution. All rights reserved. Reproduced by permission.

As you read, consider the following questions:

1. According to Revere, what achievements had there been in US-North Korean talks just before Kim Jong-il's death?

2. What examples does Revere give to show that provocations are part of North Korea's negotiating strategy?

3. Why does Revere say that it is unacceptable to give up the goal of denuclearization?

When North Korean leader Kim Jong-il suddenly died on December 17, 2011, U.S. and North Korean nuclear negotiators were reportedly preparing for a bilateral meeting in Beijing to discuss a possible return to multilateral denuclearization talks in the coming year. That meeting, now postponed, would have been the third in a series that began with a late-July encounter in New York City. The New York meeting between then U.S. special envoy for North Korea policy Stephen W. Bosworth and DPRK [the Democratic People's Republic of Korea, also known as North Korea] first vice foreign minister Kim Kye-gwan re-established a senior diplomatic channel that had been suspended for almost 18 months.

Kim's Demise and U.S.-North Korean Talks

After the New York meeting, U.S. and North Korean defense officials met in Bangkok on October 21 and quickly agreed to resume joint efforts to recover the remains of American troops missing in the Korean War. Only days later came another round of senior-level diplomatic talks, this time in Geneva, October 24–25. Ambassador Bosworth called the discussions "very positive and generally constructive" and noted that the two sides had "narrowed" some differences and "explored" other areas of disagreement. Bosworth added that the two sides had made progress in discussing "what has to be done before we can both agree to a resumption of the Six-Party Talks" [between North Korea, South Korea, China, Japan, Russia, and the United States].

After stepping down as special envoy after the Geneva talks, Bosworth was much more positive, saying he expected a resumption of "formal dialogue with the North Koreans on issues of substance sometime in the relatively near future, both perhaps bilaterally, but also in the multilateral Six-Party Talks." Bosworth's statement was the clearest indication to date that the two sides were on a trajectory that could eventually lead to renewed multilateral talks.

The bilateral dialogue reached a new stage when, the day before Kim's death, U.S. special envoy for human rights in North Korea Robert King concluded two days of talks with his DPRK counterpart in Beijing about the resumption of U.S. food aid. The December 15–16 talks followed a May visit by King to Pyongyang—the first time a U.S. human rights envoy had ever been received in North Korea.

News of King's Beijing discussions was eclipsed by the announcement of Kim Jong-il's death, but it was clear that the two sides had come close to an agreement under which the United States would provide 240,000 metric tons of monitored "nutritional assistance" to the most vulnerable people in North Korea. In return, North Korea would agree to freeze operation of the uranium enrichment facility at its Yongbyon nuclear complex, allow International Atomic Energy Agency (IAEA) monitors to oversee the freeze, and accept other U.S. preconditions for the resumption of multilateral denuclearization talks.

A New Ballgame After Kim's Death?

One of the first questions prompted by Kim Jong-il's death was whether the U.S.-DPRK dialogue would continue. Kim's demise prompted speculation about the imminent collapse of the North Korean regime. Some suggested that political in-fighting or even a coup might occur, or that his designated successor, Kim Jong-un, the deceased leader's youngest son, would unilaterally end talks with the United States or launch provocations to demonstrate his military leadership. Some called for the United States to back away from further talks and adopt a wait-and-see posture, suggesting that the United States would not be able to do business with the new North Korean leader.

The [President Barack] Obama administration's measured approach after Kim's death reflected a very different take on events than that contained in the speculation cited above. The U.S. response to Kim's demise included a carefully worded statement by Secretary of State [Hillary] Clinton that used the late leader's formal title, conveyed America's "thoughts and prayers" to the North Korean people, and pointed to the possibility of improved relations. After U.S. Defense Secretary Leon Panetta conferred with his South Korean counterpart, U.S. forces in the South were directed to maintain their normal alert levels. The Obama administration also wasted no time in reaching out to New York–based DPRK diplomats only two days after Kim's death to follow up the Beijing dialogue on food assistance.

Washington appears to have concluded that the new developments in North Korea do not warrant a change in the U.S. approach and that continuing the current policy, while carefully observing North Korean behavior after Kim's death, represents the best path forward for now. There is an expectation in Washington that there will be continuity in the North, at least in the near term.

This judgment is based on several factors, one of which is the understanding that Kim Jong-un has been part of the DPRK decision-making process that had approved the North's outreach to Washington (and Seoul) in recent months. Washington has probably also assessed that the new leader will avoid raising questions about his father's legacy by making any significant departures from his father's policies for now. Washington also understands that the two key institutions in North Korea—the military and the party—both endorsed the young Kim's leadership precisely because he is his father's son, underscoring the fact that all political legitimacy in the DPRK derives from continuing this all-important family tie.

The administration knows that the young Kim's succession had been carefully charted for more than three years since his father suffered a stroke in the summer of 2008. And they are aware that, since the announcement of Kim Jong-il's death, we have been observing the implementation of an elaborate game plan that was long in the making, even if the suddenness of Kim's death may not have given the regime all the time it may have wanted to refine the plan. Washington's cautious outreach to the North after Kim's death probably reflected a decision to carefully test the waters in Pyongyang to confirm these judgments. . . .

Why Talks?—The U.S. Position

What has prompted the United States to explore a possible return to multilateral talks with Pyongyang? A key factor is concern over the possibility of military confrontation with the DPRK. The provocations of 2010 were serious, and in certain respects without precedent. The torpedoing of the *Cheonan* took place in South Korean waters and killed 46 South Korean sailors—the largest death toll of any military incident since the Korean War. The artillery attack on Yeonpyeong Island was a major violation of the Korean War armistice agreement, and the first time that the North's artillery shelled South Korean territory since the Korean War.

After the attack on Yeonpyeong, U.S. and ROK [Republic of Korea, or South Korea] forces sent a strong deterrent message to the North. Nevertheless, the boldness of the attack, as well as its potential to escalate into a broader conflict, unnerved Washington. Because of the attack, South Korea adopted new rules of engagement that made it virtually certain that it would carry out a vigorous military response to a new North Korean attack. This raised the stakes in any future provocation by Pyongyang.

Administration contacts have told me that the danger posed by this situation encouraged the view that one way of reducing the possibility of North Korean provocations was to get Pyongyang "invested" in a dialogue process that could yield significant benefits and make clear to the DPRK what it would lose if it carried out new attacks. Being at the table with the DPRK could also offer useful insights into the North's thinking that could help anticipate its behavior. And having a reliable channel of communication is useful when dealing with an unpredictable adversary, especially if it can be used to deliver strong warnings about certain DPRK behavior.

Officials with whom I have spoken acknowledge that such an approach provides no guarantee against provocations. This is an important point, for it would be a mistake to believe that talks with North Korea can, by themselves, deter military action. In this connection, some have argued that North Korea does not engage in nuclear or missile provocations when it is negotiating with the United States. Such a view unfortunately overlooks the history of U.S.-DPRK diplomatic engagement as well as the nature of North Korean tactics.

For the DPRK, provocations are part of its unique approach to negotiations and are often carried out to change the dynamics during talks. In a variation on Clausewitz [referring to Carl Philipp Gottfried von Clausewitz, a Prussian military theorist famous for the statement "war is the continuation of diplomacy by other means"], the North sees provocations as the continuation of diplomacy by other means.

Examples of this occurred in the summer of 1998, when the DPRK threatened to remove and reprocess fuel rods from its 5-megawatt reactor at Yongbyon, just as discussions were under way with the United States about the October 1994 agreed framework. As those of us involved in the talks concluded at the time, the intent of this move was to pressure the United States by introducing a new threat into an ongoing negotiation. To add to the sense of crisis, the North launched a Taepodong-2 long-range missile over Japan and into the North Pacific on August 31, 1998. The launch occurred while U.S. and DPRK diplomats were discussing the North's earlier threat, and as the United States was conveying its concerns over another major challenge—the U.S. discovery of a large underground facility at Kumchangni that Washington suspected might have a nuclear role.

There is something to be said for using talks to discourage bad behavior. But we should be realistic. Relying largely on negotiations to deter the DPRK from military action would be a mistake. It could also allow North Korea to believe that the best way to get America's attention at the negotiating table is to engage in, or threaten to engage in, provocations. We saw a troubling example of this in 2006, when the United States responded to North Korea's first nuclear test by returning to the Six-Party Talks within a matter of weeks.

U.S. interest in re-engaging with North Korea is also driven by concern that, in the absence of a negotiating process, there is no practical way to restrain North Korea from expanding its nuclear and missile programs. After the [George W.] Bush administration's negotiating approach on North Korea fell apart in late 2008, nothing prevented North Korea from manufacturing new nuclear weapons or developing and testing the missile systems with which to deliver them.

North Korea exploited this opening. With its nuclear test of May 25, 2009, Pyongyang demonstrated how quickly it could resume work on developing a more sophisticated plutonium-based nuclear weapon. After the collapse of the Six-Party Talks, Pyongyang revealed a new capability— uranium enrichment—that sent the international community a stark message that the DPRK now had a second path to nuclear weapons development.

Pyongyang revealed this capability—one that the United States had long suspected the DPRK was secretly developing—to U.S. nuclear weapons expert Dr. Siegfried Hecker and a visiting delegation in November 2010. The revelation served to dramatically underscore the fact that the Obama administration's policy approach was not meeting the goal of ending the North Korean nuclear program.

Critics of the Obama administration have made much of this failure. They have focused in particular on the administration's policy of "strategic patience," which has held that the United States would not rush back into negotiations until the DPRK changed its behavior. While this approach had insulated the administration from charges it was entering into unproductive negotiations, it has also opened it up to criticism from both supporters and opponents of dialogue with Pyongyang. Each group, for very different reasons, has accused the administration of ignoring the threat posed by the North's growing nuclear and missile capabilities.

Nothing in the aftermath of Kim Jong-il's death appears to have changed the basic U.S. calculus behind its interest in re-engagement with the DPRK, even if there are uncertainties about the North's new leader and concerns about the future stability of the regime. The potential for military provocation remains a worry, but Washington may see renewed dialogue as a useful way of warning the new leadership in Pyongyang about the consequences of adventurism. The Obama administration may also view Kim's death as an opportunity to urge the North's emerging leadership to change its position on nuclear weapons and missiles. At a minimum, Washington may want to use new talks to explore how post–Kim Jong-il politics are affecting the North's negotiating behavior. . . .

Why Re-Engage?

Despite the downbeat prospects, there is good reason to re-engage with the North on nuclear matters, despite our doubts about Pyongyang's intentions. Complete denuclearization of North Korea may not be possible now and, as many believe, could be impossible as long as the current regime is in power. But giving up on this goal is unacceptable. Doing so would send a dangerous signal to our allies and partners that we are prepared to accept for the long haul North Korea's possession of nuclear weapons. It would seriously damage the international nonproliferation regime. And it would inadvertently help legitimize North Korea's longtime pursuit of nuclear weapons and violation of its bilateral and multilateral obligations.

At the same time, leaving in place an unconstrained DPRK nuclear program undermines the U.S., ROK, Japanese, and Chinese interest in a stable and predictable Northeast Asia. An agreement or series of steps that imposes meaningful constraints on this program and lays the groundwork for complete denuclearization would reduce the current level of danger and be in our collective interests. An agreement that merely freezes North Korea's programs in their present state would not be.

While pursuing the complete denuclearization of North Korea, there are goals short of full denuclearization that could be achieved in the near term. One of these is the elimination of the remaining elements of North Korea's plutonium-based nuclear program at Yongbyon, including the 5-megawatt reactor, the fuel fabrication and reprocessing facilities, and the fresh fuel for this reactor and a 50-megawatt reactor on which construction has been halted. Existing six-party agreements call for these facilities to be frozen, disabled, and eventually dismantled. Any new negotiation should hold Pyongyang to the commitments it has made to do so.

Ironically, Pyongyang's success with uranium enrichment may make this goal more attainable if the North comes to the table prepared to negotiate away its plutonium production program in the belief that it has a reliable alternate route to nuclear weapons via uranium enrichment. Even if it does and even if such a negotiation succeeds, it will still leave U.S. negotiators with a daunting task. Eliminating the North's plutonium-based program at a known location has proven terribly difficult to achieve over the past 17 years. Even tougher will be the complete elimination of a uranium-based nuclear weapons program that can be easily hidden and about which we know little ..., but we must nonetheless try, initially by seeking to dismantle those elements that have already been revealed to us.

This process should begin with North Korea's acceptance of a monitored freeze of its uranium enrichment facility at Yongbyon—one of the United States' pre-steps. There are signs that the DPRK might accept this. Moving beyond a freeze to the dismantlement of this facility will be more problematic, but it must be a central focus of six-party negotiations, as should putting in place an agreed process to deal with other enrichment activities that may be discovered later.

"The talks themselves exemplify how, for almost a decade, Washington has followed Beijing's Korea policy as if it were its own."

Talks with North Korea Would Worsen the Nuclear Threat

John R. Bolton

John R. Bolton is a diplomat and former US ambassador to the United Nations. In the following viewpoint, he argues that restarting the Six-Party Talks—with North Korea, South Korea, China, Japan, Russia, and the United States—would be a sign of weakness and would simply empower the North Korean regime. Instead, he argues, the United States should isolate North Korea by cutting off its access to financial markets and goods. He also suggests planning for the transition to a unified Korea so that the United States will be ready when the North's totalitarian government collapses.

As you read, consider the following questions:

1. What other rogue regime does Bolton say is connected to North Korea, and what evidence does he present for this contention?

John R. Bolton, "North Korea: Not the Time for Talks," *The Wall Street Journal*, January 3, 2011. Reproduced by permission.

2. What preparations does Bolton say that the United States should make for North Korea's fall?

3. How does Bolton say that China's attitudes toward North Korea may be altering?

President Obama's North Korea policy has come to an entirely predictable dead end. Having for two years correctly resisted resuming the Six-Party Talks on the North's nuclear-weapons program, Mr. Obama is now pressuring South Korea to do just that. This is a significant mistake. It would have been bad enough had Mr. Obama simply picked up where the Bush administration left off in January 2009, but restarting the talks now will signal weakness and indecisiveness.

Since Mr. Obama's inauguration, Pyongyang has detonated its second nuclear device and launched two unprovoked military attacks—torpedoing a South Korean naval vessel last March and shelling Yeonpyeong Island in November, killing several civilians. Even more significant was the revelation of large, sophisticated uranium-enrichment facilities at Yongbyon, and construction there of a new nuclear reactor to replace the existing aged facility.

Resuming the Six-Party Talks, which include the two Koreas, China, Japan, Russia and America, clearly has global ramifications. Pyongyang and Tehran have cooperated closely on ballistic missiles and almost certainly on nuclear matters, as the North's construction of a reactor in Syria, destroyed by Israel in 2007, demonstrates. It has long been a mistake to treat these rogue states as unrelated threats, a point that still eludes the Obama administration.

The talks themselves exemplify how, for almost a decade, Washington has followed Beijing's Korea policy as if it were its own. China does not want a bellicose, nuclear North Korea destabilizing East Asia, prompting Japan and others to seek nuclear weapons. But it has definitely prized the North as a buffer state against U.S. forces in the South. China would pre-

The Korean Demilitarized Zone (DMZ)

TAKEN FROM: "Korean Demilitarized Zone," Korean DMZ, June 28, 2009. koreandmz.org.

fer a nonnuclear North Korea but has feared to act on that goal lest the North itself collapse and the Koreas reunify. The talks are Beijing's mechanism for maintaining the uneasy equilibrium of its contradictory policies, and keeping both the U.S. and North Korea in line.

While South Koreans seem increasingly to be rejecting the six-party approach because of the North's aggression, Mr. Obama is working hard to squeeze President Lee Myung-bak to accept reopening the talks. Last Wednesday before a foreign-affairs meeting, Mr. Lee said his country has "no choice but to resolve the problem of dismantling North Korea's nuclear program diplomatically through the Six-Party Talks." But his administration has yet to agree to a resumption of talks. Mr. Obama's representatives are descending on Seoul, Beijing and Tokyo this week and next to torque up the pressure.

Washington should advocate America's interests rather than China's. Our objective should be to increase pressure on Kim Jong-il's regime, hopefully leading to its collapse.

We should thoroughly isolate North Korea by denying it access to international financial markets, ramping up efforts to prevent trade in weapons-related materials and pressuring China to adhere to existing U.N. sanctions resolutions. Opening North Korea to foreign commerce to benefit its near-starving population, as some advocate, is utterly fanciful. If the regime had ever cared about its people, they wouldn't be in such dire straits.

We should also dramatically expand preparations for Kim's inevitable demise. It is a self-fulfilling prophecy for Washington to see his death only as a risk, rather than an opportunity. We should take every advantage of the inevitable rivalry and confusion that will accompany the transition, and use whatever levers are available to undermine the regime. We must also plan to meet the North's evident humanitarian needs, whether or not there are massive refugee flows. Even if the population stayed put after a regime collapse, the North's misery would still require urgent attention. And we must ensure that the North's weapons of mass destruction do not fall into the wrong hands.

Many of China's younger leaders do not reflexively support Pyongyang. Although their elders may be hopeless on the subject, the rising policy makers must hear from us that peacefully reunifying Korea is in Beijing's long-term interests. Having a puppet state separating China from U.S. forces may once have been attractive, but forward-looking Chinese should not accept defending the North's appalling record. This will be a hard conversation, but we have never had meaningful discussions with China on reunifying the Koreas.

While Mr. Obama is unlikely to shift his views voluntarily, Washington's politics changed dramatically in November while Pyongyang was attacking the South and showing off its nuclear wares. After 10 years of error, we should recognize, better late than never, that unifying Korea is key to Asian peace and stability.

| "Given its status as an impartial outsider, the [European Union] can play a uniquely constructive role in the multilateral talks for denuclearizing North Korea."

European Participation in Talks Could Reduce the North Korean Nuclear Threat

Philip Worré and Intaek Han

Philip Worré is the executive director of International Security Information Services (ISIS) Europe; Intaek Han is a policy advisor to the South Korean Ministry of Foreign Affairs and associate research fellow at the Jeju Peace Institute (JPI). In the following viewpoint, the authors argue that the European Union (EU) should be included in the Six-Party Talks, which include North Korea, South Korea, China, Japan, Russia, and the United States. The authors say that EU countries have long been engaged in relations with North Korea. Moreover, the EU has vital interests in the Northeast Asia region. The authors conclude that the EU's presence as a neutral observer might help break the talks out of stalemate and could lead to progress in negotiations.

As you read, consider the following questions:

1. According to the authors, the EU has participated in what regional efforts to denuclearize North Korea?

2. What unique challenges do the authors say the current situation presents to the EU?

3. How much humanitarian and development aid has been provided by the EU to North Korea?

The Six-Party Talks [with North Korea, South Korea, Russia, China, Japan, and the United States] are stalled and it is not clear when they will resume. Critics argue that the talks have achieved little in their efforts to denuclearise North Korea.

Add the European Union

Such criticism may be valid seeing how the talks did not prevent North Korea from conducting nuclear tests or launching long-range missiles. Still, the Six-Party Talks are the only currently available diplomatic vehicle to resolve the North Korean nuclear crisis. While they may not deliver results in the immediate future, these talks are likely to continue given the interest in denuclearising North Korea.

The EU [European Union] takes part in multilateral sanctions against North Korea, but is not currently a member of the Six-Party Talks. There is no compelling reason why the EU should not be a party to the talks. The EU has recently demonstrated a keen interest in deepening its involvement in East Asia; and becoming an observer in the Six-Party Talks would allow the EU to act as an objective, helpful, and mutually acceptable broker, who could actively avoid the difficulties and frustrations the forum has met with in the past.

The EU has participated in regional efforts to denuclearise North Korea before: It was a board member of the now-defunct Korean Peninsula Energy Development Organization

(KEDO) and has regularly engaged in political dialogue with the DPRK [Democratic People's Republic of Korea, or North Korea] since 2001, when it established formal diplomatic ties.

The EU's member states share the common goal of achieving a lasting peace. To this effect, the EU has developed expertise in promoting democratic processes, reforming the security sector, and developing inclusive solutions to long-standing problems, with a focus on security and defence issues. The EU also has a long history of promoting diplomatic negotiations to solve major issues, and is well regarded as such.

France, Germany and the UK are currently involved in the 'Five Plus One' negotiations with Iran (also known as 'E3 plus 3'); at times they have been seen to adopt 'hawkish' attitudes. Yet it is unlikely that the EU joining the Six-Party Talks would create the same problem, because a majority of EU member states also have diplomatic relations with the DPRK, and some have a long history of involvement in DPRK-related negotiations. Sweden, for example, has five representatives stationed at Panmunjom as members of the Neutral Nations Supervisory Commission (NNSC), and Poland also attends some NNSC meetings, through South Korea.

Aiding New Discussions

The current situation in East Asia presents unique challenges for the EU, such as the ongoing China-US struggle for regional hegemony. The complex relationships between the parties involved, and the potential repercussions for the North Korea debate, could make it difficult for the EU to maintain a strong level of credibility in negotiations and in the region in general. The position adopted by some EU member states at the 'Five Plus One' talks with Iran may either prevent proper negotiations with the DPRK or highlight possible contradictions in various countries' stances.

If the EU joins the talks as an observer, it could act as a buffer between the other six parties: The EU has a history of providing humanitarian and development aid to the DPRK (over €366 million since 1995; equivalent to US$458 million), it has know-how in cultivating multilateralism, it favours a 'soft power' approach (as opposed to NATO's [North Atlantic Treaty Organization's] more 'traditional power' style), and does not have a military presence in East Asia.

In a deadlock situation, where negotiations are difficult because of the deeply entrenched political positions of different parties, an additional actor could facilitate new discussions. Given its status as an impartial outsider, the EU can play a uniquely constructive role in the multilateral talks for denuclearising North Korea. The proposal for 'Six Plus One' talks is therefore worth considering.

Periodical and Internet Sources Bibliography

The following articles have been selected to supplement the diverse views presented in this chapter.

Victor Asal and Bryan Early	"Are We Focusing on the Wrong Nuclear Threat?," *Foreign Policy*, May 24, 2012.
Maggie Beidelman	"Stanford Professor: N. Korea Nuclear Threat Overplayed," PaloAltoPatch, November 30, 2010.
Jimmy Carter	"North Korea Wants to Make a Deal," *New York Times*, September 15, 2010.
Hyung-Jim Kim and Foster Klug	"South Korea: North Korea Leadership Transition Must Bring Peace," *Huffington Post*, January 2, 2012.
Bruce Klingner	"Uncertainties over North Korea's Leadership Transition: Broader Contingency Planning Is Essential for Regional Stability," Heritage Foundation Backgrounder, no. 2678, April 10, 2012.
Jeffrey Kluger	"Kim's Rocket Fails, but North Korea's Space Threat Is Scarier than You Think," *Time*, April 12, 2012.
Jean H. Lee	"North Korea Farm Reforms: First Step to a Market Economy?," *Christian Science Monitor*, September 24, 2012.
Xiaodon Liang	"The Six-Party Talks at a Glance," Arms Control Association, May 2012.
Joshua Philipp	"Difficulties Ahead in North Korea's Leadership Transition," *Epoch Times*, September 30, 2010.
Daniel Pinkston	"A Revival of the Six-Party Talks? Four Steps the DPRK Can Take to Resuscitate Diplomacy," International Crisis Group, July 26, 2011.

What Are Human Rights Issues in North and South Korea?

Chapter Preface

North Korea has one of the worst human rights records in the world. However, South Korea—like most nations—also has human rights issues. One of the most controversial of these has been its treatment of members of the Falun Gong movement.

Falun Gong is a spiritual movement centered around meditation and exercise. It was founded in China in the early 1990s. The Chinese Communist government, which opposes any religious or popular movement not sanctioned by the state, has violently repressed Falun Gong, imprisoning and allegedly torturing adherents.

Some Falun Gong adherents have tried to escape persecution in China by seeking political refuge in South Korea. However, in part at the urging of China, South Korea has in many cases refused to grant asylum to these refugees. According to Evan Ramstad in a September 20, 2011, article in the *Wall Street Journal*, South Korea deported ten Falun Gong practitioners to China between 2009 and 2011. More than forty other Chinese Falun Gong members were denied asylum during the same period.

Ramstad reported that numerous human rights groups protested Korea's actions. The groups argued that returning Falun Gong members to China violated South Korea's treaty obligations with the United Nation (UN). For example, the UN convention against torture prevents signatories from transferring individuals to a country where they are likely to be subject to inhumane treatment.

South Korea policy toward Falun Gong refugees may be changing, however. In a July 16, 2012, article in the *Epoch Times*, Kim Guk Hwan and Moon Yong Han reported that the Supreme Court of Korea had ruled in favor of a Falun Gong practitioner. The practitioner, Mr. Shen, was therefore allowed to stay in South Korea, becoming the first member of Falun Gong to be granted asylum in the country. The Supreme Court specifically rejected South Korea's claim that "only main coordinators of Falun Gong" faced persecution, instead affirming that "in China, the persecution against Falun Gong practitioners is still ongoing," and that "the [Chinese] government attitude towards the group has not changed at all."

While the status of Falun Gong refugees may have been at least provisionally resolved by the Korean Supreme Court decision, other human rights issues on the Korean Peninsula continue to be controversial. This chapter examines a number of these controversies in both South and North Korea.

| *"One tells of a female guard who took glee in beating prisoners with lumber."*

South Korea Has Exposed Human Rights Abuses in North Korean Prison Camps

Chico Harlan

Chico Harlan is a foreign correspondent for the Washington Post. *In the following viewpoint, he discusses a new South Korean report that details abuses in North Korea's network of prison camps. According to the report, from 150,000 to 200,000 prisoners are kept in these camps, where they are routinely starved and tortured. Harlan says that it is hoped that the report can be used at a later time to hold accountable those in North Korea who are responsible for these systemic human rights violations.*

As you read, consider the following questions:

1. Why do human rights activists believe South Korea has legal standing to convene a tribunal on northern prison camps, according to Harlan?

2. What abuses does Harlan describe at the Yodok prison camp?

3. According to Kim Gang-il, how were dead bodies treated at Yodok prison camp?

A South Korean government-funded human rights group has released a series of raw firsthand accounts of North Korea's political prison camps, Seoul's first comprehensive attempt to catalogue the atrocities that Pyongyang denies take place.

Accountable for Their Crimes

The 381-page report, based on about 200 face-to-face interviews with defectors who survived the camps, is a significant step for a South Korean government that has long remained quiet about the human rights abuses of its neighbor.

The report, issued last week [in May 2012] with little fanfare, provides a record of what its authors say are specific international human rights violations, including where and when they occurred. Although names have been redacted, the report has biographical information on North Korean agents and prison guards who allegedly oversaw the abuses, providing the potential foundation for Seoul to one day convene a tribunal that prosecutes those responsible.

Some human rights activists have requested that Seoul do as much, because South Korea's constitution stipulates that North Koreans are entitled to be citizens of the South, with legal standing in the court system.

Even the threat of such trials would put North Korean authorities on notice "that they will be held accountable for their crimes," said Suzanne Scholte, chairman of the North Korea Freedom Coalition, which works to promote human rights in North Korea.

"The reason we published this," said Lee Yong-ken, chief of the North Korea human rights team at the National Human Rights Commission of Korea, which compiled the report, "is to spread awareness and to have a realistic account."

The political prison camps—known in the North as "totally controlled zones"—and reformation camps, meant for less serious offenders, together underpin the system of surveillance and punishment that the ruling Kim family has used for decades to snuff out dissent and threats to its power. North Korea officially denies the existence of such camps, but the city-size installations are visible by satellite imagery, and independent human rights reports suggest that 150,000 to 200,000 people are confined within them.

Despite more than a decade of reports from human rights organizations about the camps, the outside world has almost no record of the specifics: who is there, why they are there, and what their lives are like.

But the steady flow of defectors into South Korea is providing Seoul with a growing opportunity to change that. Roughly 23,500 of them now live in the South, including at least several hundred former prisoners.

Detailed Testimony

After a year of interviews, the commission published defectors' accounts almost verbatim. Defectors describe their own experiences and the things they witnessed. One tells of a female guard who took glee in beating prisoners with lumber. Another tells of a 19-year-old who was executed by a 21-year-old guard, brains blown up so "severely that the face was unrecognizable." Yet another describes torture methods, including what prisoners called the "Flying Jet," the "Motorcycle" and "Pumping." While subjected to such torture, detainees, during mealtime, were given spoons with the narrow tips removed, making it harder for them to swallow the utensils and commit suicide.

Some of the most detailed testimony comes from Jeong Gwang-il, who says he spent three years (2000–2003) at the Yodok prison camp after illegally crossing into China.

At Yodok, perpetually famished prisoners sometimes participated in Olympic-style games, ordered as amusement for agents from the "integrity department." Those agents, according to Jeong's testimony, sent prisoners on 2.5-mile downhill races to retrieve corn cakes at the bottom.

"Many prisoners fell off the cliff while hustling and jostling on the way," the report says, "and the integrity department agents considered this as a spectacle or entertainment."

At Yodok, laborers who failed to meet work quotas saw their meager food rations cut in half, a cycle that led to starvation because the less they ate, the weaker they got, and the poorer they became at work.

During corn farming season in April, prisoners were asked to mix corn seeds with human feces, reducing the motivation for thieves to eat them. One prisoner, Jeong testified, stole the seeds anyway, tried to clean them and died of colitis.

Those who complained about conditions were frequently betrayed by fellow prisoners, Jeong said in a separate interview last week at a coffee shop in Seoul. Often, Jeong himself informed guards about such misbehavior. "Some people would say, 'This is worse than being dead.' And I'd report it. Then the person would be taken to solitary confinement for one month and given one meal per day."

Jeong, slim and fit, spoke matter-of-factly about the rules of the camp, where you told on others to avoid punishment for yourself. "It sounds brutal," he said, "but that's the way it worked."

"Assailants" Listed

Many of the defector testimonies are accompanied by a list of "assailants"—that is, authorities who, survivors say, committed the abuses. In the case of defector Kim Gang-il, for instance,

North Korean Prison and Labor Camps

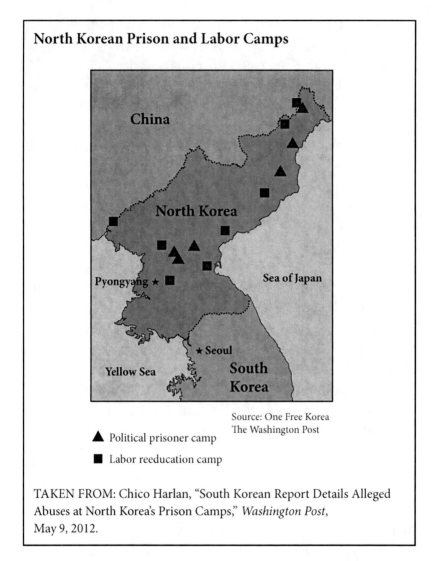

Source: One Free Korea
The Washington Post

▲ Political prisoner camp

■ Labor reeducation camp

TAKEN FROM: Chico Harlan, "South Korean Report Details Alleged Abuses at North Korea's Prison Camps," *Washington Post*, May 9, 2012.

the assailants include the preliminary judge who sentenced him, members of the central prosecutor's office, a major general at the reformation camp and other security officials. The names have been redacted from the report, but the commission has them on file.

Kim, according to his testimony, was arrested in 2004 for "illegal smuggling" after trying to sell copper to China. He said he was beaten and tortured at a detention house and then sent to a mountainous reformation camp, where prisoners slept 60 or 70 to a room. Many worked in copper mines that had no safety lights and where high-tension wires passed "chaotically." Workers "frequently" died of electrocution.

Those who died from infectious disease, starvation or labor were often not immediately buried, according to Kim. Rats devoured the corpses' eyes, ears and genitals, "making them impossible to recognize."

Eventually, the bodies were dumped into a "large steel furnace in a place inside the camp called 'Bulmangsan' and burned . . . with logs."

But the incinerators didn't burn the bodies completely and were always filled with charred skeletal remains. Workers used the ashes of the corpses as fertilizer for pumpkins, radishes and cabbage.

Those vegetables, Kim said, "grew well where they sprinkled the ashes."

"South Korea should abolish or revise the National Security Law to ensure that it fully protects the freedom of opinion and expression."

South Korea's National Security Law Violates Human Rights

Kay Seok

Kay Seok is the North Korea researcher for Human Rights Watch. In the following viewpoint, she reports on the arrest of a South Korean who had visited North Korea and extolled the North's virtues. Seok argues that South Korea's National Security Law has been used to arrest and prosecute South Koreans who speak in favor of the North. Seok notes that North Korea's human rights record is much worse than South Korea's, but she says that this is no excuse for the South to limit freedom of expression. She urges the abolition of the South's National Security Law and says that the South should respect freedom of speech.

As you read, consider the following questions:

1. What actions by Reverend Han Sang-ryul does Seok consider "unconscionable" and why?

2. What websites does Seok say that South Korea blocks under its National Security Law?

3. Under what circumstances does Seok say a nation may reasonably limit freedom of speech?

A sense of déjà vu emanated from recent South-North border events: another imprisoned American left the North with a former U.S. president, and another South Korean was arrested upon return from the North for violating the National Security Law.

Restricting Free Speech

South Korea's prosecutors indicted Rev. Han Sang-ryul on Sept. 9, [2010,] accusing him of praising North Korea and denouncing South Korea during a 70-day visit to the North, which began in June.

Few would dispute that Rev. Han, a man of faith, apparently maintained an unconscionable silence about the plight of his fellow Christians in North Korea during his visit. In doing so, he chose to ignore the North Korean government's brutal persecution of Christians and members of any other religious faith outside of state control.

Han's participation in such North Korean propaganda only discredits him. Frankly, it's hard to see why anyone would take him—or the vitriolic North Korean propaganda that spews forth daily from the KCNA [Korean Central News Agency]—seriously.

Yet the South Korean government doesn't see it that way. Rev. Han was arrested as soon as he returned on Aug. 20, fresh from his send-off at a farewell party organized by the North Korean government, reportedly featuring 200 singing and chanting well-wishers.

By arresting him, South Korean authorities are clearly violating his right to peacefully exercise the right to freedom of expression. They are also rescuing Rev. Han's reputation by making him a martyr and increasing his value to North Korea's propagandists.

In late August, South Korea unapologetically blocked access to North Korea's propaganda-filled Facebook and Twitter accounts. The operators of Facebook later closed North Korea's account for still unexplained violations of its regulations.

The Twitter account is evidently still operating, though blocked in South Korea. The South Korean government has previously blocked virtually all other Web sites considered pro–North Korea.

These are just the latest episodes in the South Korean government's opportunistic use of the National Security Law to severely restrict the right to freedom of expression. Under the law, South Koreans are barred from meeting with North Koreans or visiting North Korea without state permission. They are forbidden from praising North Korea or disseminating North Korean propaganda.

The law clearly violates South Korea's international human rights obligations.

Just as the government should not arrest people for joining a cult, neither should it incarcerate them for praising North Korea. Even when certain beliefs or thoughts appear wrong, bizarre or disturbing, propounding them should be protected as long as such speech does not amount to incitement, violence or other criminal action.

But according to the 2009 U.S. Department of State Human Rights Report, South Korea prosecuted 34 persons for violating the law in 2009, an increase from 27 in 2008.

Abolish or Revise

The South Korean government should abolish or revise its National Security Law to protect freedom of expression, a basic human right enshrined in the Universal Declaration of Human Rights. South Korea is also a state party to the Inter-

The Conflict over the National Security Law

[There has been a] heated confrontation between those who support and those who oppose the National Security Law [in South Korea]. Since the democratic transition in 1987, there have been various attempts to eliminate the National Security Law, which had been often abused to oppress political dissidents during the authoritarian era. Liberal reunification movement activists made visits to North Korea without governmental permission in order to invalidate and demonstrate the ineffectiveness of the National Security Law. Prominent among those were novelist Hwang Sok-yong, the reverend Moon Ik-hwan, and college student Lim Su-kyung. Also, several NGOs [nongovernmental organizations] emerged that advocated the elimination of the National Security Law. In 2000, 232 progressive NGOs launched a nationwide network to eradicate the law. The network expanded, comprising 305 NGOs in 2004.

Hoon Jaung,
"The Two Tales of the Korean Presidency: Imperial but
Imperiled Presidency," in The Rule of Law in South Korea.
Eds. Jongryn Mo and David W. Brady.
Stanford, CA: Hoover Institution Press, 2009, pp. 72–73.

national Covenant on Civil and Political Rights. Article 19 of this convention stipulates that "everyone shall have the right to hold opinions without interference."

Although states can limit free expression in the interest of national security, they may do so only when "necessary in a democratic society" and for compelling reasons, such as protection of military secrets, not simply to avoid embarrassment or promote ideological solidarity.

One might argue that South Korea's arrest of Rev. Han and blocking information on the Internet pales in comparison with North Korea's approach to freedom of speech.

Very few people in North Korea have access to the Internet. And any North Korean who returned home after openly criticizing North Korea on a trip to the South would face horrifying consequences—dispatch to the infamous forced-labor camps as "traitors" or perhaps immediate execution.

But the fact that North Korea is one of the worst abusers of basic human rights and that it has kidnapped, detained and murdered many South Korean civilians, should not give South Korea carte blanche to limit South Koreans' freedom of opinion and expression. To set North Korea as the standard against which to measure civil rights is to set no standard at all for valuing human dignity and freedom.

South Korea should abolish or revise the National Security Law to ensure that it fully protects the freedom of opinion and expression. If ensuring such freedom means allowing South Koreans to see North Korea's propaganda or even to support Kim Jong-il [North Korean leader], then so be it.

That is democracy.

And democracy is what South Koreans fought so hard and long to achieve in their decades of struggle under past military dictatorships.

They deserve nothing less.

> *"In his 15 years working in human rights, he had never seen his fellow South Koreans asking about how to help."*

South Koreans Are Reluctant to Highlight North Korean Human Rights Violations

Iris Chung

Iris Chung is an American writer currently studying at Ewha Womans University in South Korea. In the following viewpoint, she discusses her trip to South Korea and her involvement in activism against North Korean human rights abuses. She says that South Koreans are generally reluctant to involve themselves in protests against North Korean abuses because they fear that such protests will anger the North and delay reconciliation and reunification. Chung also points out that, as an American, she finds it difficult to judge the South Koreans since she does not share their difficulties, their history, or their perspective.

As you read, consider the following questions:

1. According to Chung, from where is the term "Sunshine Policy" derived?

Iris Chung, "Bittersweet Longing: Fighting for North Korean Human Rights in South Korea," Matador Abroad, November 11, 2011. Copyright © 2011 by Matador Abroad. All Rights Reserved. Reproduced by permission.

2. What does "kyopo" mean, and how does it affect Chung's attitude toward activism?

3. Why did Chung's attitude toward the balloon launch change?

During my early days exploring Insadong, one of the city's [Seoul's] traditional tourist traps, I was surprised when an American handed me a flier about the state of human rights in North Korea. In addition to being a white guy in Asia, he looked particularly out of place among the usual street vendors peddling snacks and handicrafts. He stood with a handful of Americans and Koreans among several large poster boards that displayed pictures of skeletal children. Curious, I asked him what kind of reaction he usually got from South Koreans he approached.

Human Rights, Not Reunification

"They're surprised to see a foreigner standing there," he admitted. "They won't get involved, but they say, 'Thank you for doing this.'"

He introduced himself as Dan, the international campaign director of Justice for North Korea (JFNK), a grassroots activist organization. I pushed on—had he ever had any unpleasant experiences? Wasn't the topic of reunification a controversial one?

"I care about human rights in North Korea," he said. "That doesn't necessarily mean 'reunification.'"

Apparently, it was a common misconception.

"We get some strong reactions from the street campaign," Dan acknowledged, and described a former clash with an older Korean man, "who was probably of the Sunshine Policy and very much in our face."

The Sunshine Policy started in 1998 under [South Korean] President Kim Dae-jung, resulting in an inter-Korean summit with [North Korean leader] Kim Jong-il in 2000. Instead of pushing for immediate reunification through the collapse of the North, the Sunshine Policy encourages a more gentle integration to break North Korea's isolation. The term is originally derived from Aesop's Fables, in which the Sun wins an argument with the North Wind about which is stronger. The story's moral that "persuasion is better than force" is the underlying philosophy of the Sunshine Policy, which aims to achieve peaceful coexistence between the two Koreas "through reconciliation, cooperation, and mutual exchange." Under this policy, South Korea has provided substantial economic and diplomatic aid to North Korea in order to better its relationship and to achieve political stability under present conditions.

Skirting Human Rights Violations

One aspect of the Sunshine Policy involved censoring talk of human rights violations to avoid threatening the North-South relationship and to maintain engagement with North Korea. Kim Dae-jung's avoidance of addressing human rights issues in the North set the tone for the Sunshine era. Many South Koreans felt hostile towards the George [W.] Bush administration for its strong stance against North Korea, fearing that condemning the regime would lead to conflict.

The Sunshine Policy came to an end under South Korea's current conservative administration run by President Lee Myung-bak, who opposed providing aid to the North while it was developing nuclear weapons. Last year's incidents [in 2010] involving the sinking of the navy corvette *Cheonan* and the shelling of Yeonpyeong Island also did much to cool inter-Korean relations. South Korea stopped most cross-border trade and severed all economic ties to North Korea, demanding it to own up to the unprovoked attacks and the death of 50 people.

For average citizens, the *Cheonan* and Yeonpyeong Island incidents challenged their belief that improving North-South relations through the Sunshine Policy would eventually lead to reunification. For these reasons, the question of how to improve human rights in North Korea remains one of the most polarizing and controversial issues among South Koreans. The North Korean Human Rights Act (NKHRA), for example, is a bill that has been stalled in the National Assembly since last year due to opposition from liberal parties, who view bringing light to the issue as threatening to North Korea. Under the NKHR Act, an independent body would monitor North Korean human rights and offer support to activists in the South. The U.S. and Japan passed their own versions of the bill in 2006.

Dan recalled how the man had criticized the group's posters that depicted human rights atrocities, claiming the photos of starved North Korean victims were taken over ten years ago, during the famine of the 90s.

"I couldn't catch the rest of what he said," continued Dan. "But he kept repeating, weh guk sah lam."

Although weh guk sah lam isn't a derogatory term—it simply means "foreigner"—I wondered about the old man's aggravation towards the sight of an outsider getting involved in national politics. When activist slogans claim, "Silence Kills North Koreans," where is the boundary for foreigners to remain silent? . . .

Expat Activism

As a kyopo, or the term used for those of Korean descent living abroad, I am technically not considered a weh guk sah lam. Being U.S. born and bred, I am seen as neither quite South Korean nor quite American; the legacy of a kyopo is split into two. My ambivalence towards expat activism stems from the duality of this identity. I don't want to be that self-righteous, condescending American who tells South Koreans what they should do, how they should feel, what they should care about. Yet that is often how I feel when acknowledging the reality that many South Koreans feel indifference towards matters up North.

Despite the fact that what I knew about North Korea came from a handful of articles and documentaries I'd seen prior to my arrival in Seoul, I landed convinced I wanted to help. An initial Google search led me to find "Helping Hands Korea," a Christian-based NGO [nongovernmental organization] led by director Tim Peters that provides famine relief to North Korea, as well as support to North Korean refugees in China. When I joined the group's weekly meeting, Tim shared photos from his recent visit to an orphanage in China. Surrounded by the soft lilt of Midwestern voices, gazing at a tapestry backdrop of Jesus and his disciples at the Last Supper, I felt like I'd been transported to the suburbs. The nearby pile of savory Korean snacks looked colorful and out of place. Tim and his wife, who was South Korean, were kind, encouraging me to ask questions. By Tim's estimates, more than 80% of his organization's funding came from Europe, with 10% from the U.S., and 5% from South Korea.

"Foreigners can't keep doing it themselves," he said. "It's not sustainable."

Despite a growing number of South Korean organizations championing North Korean human rights, veteran locals I'd met in seasoned activist circles attested to the overwhelming apathy of their countrymen. At a volunteer orientation session run by Justice for North Korea, only six of the 25 or so new members were South Korean. The all-day event included lectures from a host of organizations, offering a comprehensive crash course for those of us—Korean Americans, white Americans, Europeans, South Koreans—who'd arrived with a cursory understanding of human rights in the DPRK [Democratic People's Republic of Korea, or North Korea].

Sang Hun Kim, representing the North Korean Human Rights Database Center, explained the NGO's mission to investigate and collect testimonies from North Korean defectors to serve as evidence to bring forth to the U.N. [United Nations] Security Council. Previous efforts to establish a government-supported North Korean human rights record depository had been rejected for fear it "would obstruct inter-Korean peace and cooperation."

"You must shout," Sang Hun said. "But shouting won't do anything." In his 15 years working in human rights, he had never seen his fellow South Koreans asking about how to help, lamenting, "They have absolutely no interest in the situation. . . . I think South Koreans someday will have to be punished for not doing anything. For not having helped their brothers and sisters."

The founder and director of JFNK, Peter Jung, told us about crimes of the boh-ui-boo, or North Korean intelligence agency. Peter, who was imprisoned a year and a half in China for assisting defectors, continues to personally help them escape through China and Vietnam. Those who are caught, he explained, face severe penalty at North Korean prison camps. Many die due to the combination of malnutrition and forced labor of dragging tree logs and carrying 20 kg [kilogram] blocks. Some officers even examine women's "virginal parts," suspicious they might be hiding money inside of their vagina.

As he shared a book of illustrations showing the brutal torture occurring at North Korean prison camps, we gaped at sketches of people being stripped naked and beaten with sticks; suffering while their hands and legs were cut off; eating snakes and mice amongst piles of rotting corpses; running in place to stay alive while locked in a freezing room.

In one scene, a clearly pregnant woman lay flat with her back on the ground, a wooden board balanced on the top of her swelling stomach. At an officer's command, a man jumped on top of the board to smash her baby.

I'd assumed that South Koreans might have already been exposed to such images, but another volunteer told me, "As a

South Korean, I can tell you that very few have the opportunity to see the types of images you saw today."

During the break session, I eyed a tan Korean guy in a crisp, light-blue blazer standing off to the side. Approaching the microphone, he introduced himself as a colleague of Dan's at an NGO called the Network for North Korean Democracy and Human Rights. He was also a North Korean defector who had come to share his story with us, saying, "I always felt like Dan has nothing to do with North Korea ... [but it's as if he cares] more than I care. So I feel grateful. . . . Thank you for taking interest in us, when South Koreans don't."

"People are really not concerned when it comes to the North," said Yurim, a South Korean college student interning at the Ministry of Unification who I'd met outside of the session. First established in 1969, the Ministry of Unification is a government branch that works toward reunification by promoting inter-Korean dialogue, exchanges, and cooperation.

"It's common for people to say they want reunification," she said. "But a lot of [South] Koreans don't think it's good, mainly for economic reasons. Also, North Korea is the enemy. Most of my friends are against it." . . .

A Privileged Traveler

With a group of 20 others, I focused my camera lens on the stoic-faced South Korean soldier guarding the JSA. The Joint Security Area, known as the JSA, is a building where diplomatic discussions between the two countries are held; it is the only area of the DMZ [demilitarized zone between North and South Korea] within the city of Paju where South Korean and North Korean forces stand face-to-face. Although I'd circled it as a must-see destination in my Lonely Planet guidebook, South Korean civilians can only enter the JSA with special permission.

I'd nearly visited the area three months before, having heard of a "balloon launch" sending anti-North propaganda

Obscure, Inconsistent, and Absolute

Under the Kim regime [of North Korea], there is no representation of the will of the people, either as individuals or as a collective group. Kim Jong-il had the means to operate the government based on clandestine rules and orders based on his personal whim, unchecked. While Kim Jong-un may be more dependent on a collective support network, all initial indications are that he will run the regime in a similar manner. Why this system of clandestine control leads to human rights violations may be readily apparent to those who live in free societies. The will of the nation's people is neither represented in a freely elected legislative body nor in an elected executive authority; furthermore, there is no independent judiciary, so the people have no way to guarantee their rights or insist on governmental responsiveness to their concerns.

In North Korea, the leader's orders and instructions are not only absolute, but also obscure and often inconsistent. Ordinary citizens do not have access to reliable written instructions. Indeed, defining the will of the leader is itself a matter that requires an extensive bureaucracy—requiring guidance from party officials occupying a series of offices set up to promulgate instructions to sectors of the population for which they are responsible. These officials' words are themselves subject to re-interpretation by lower party officials. It is impossible for the average citizen to question what he is being told by party officials or argue that the leader actually meant something else. Often the hapless citizens of North Korea find they have offended the regime only when they have been arrested.

Ken E. Gause, Coercion, Control,
Surveillance, and Punishment: An Examination
of the North Korean Police State, *pp. 15–16.*

leaflets to North Korea from Imjingak, one of Paju's small towns located just seven kilometers from the border. I had never heard of this tactic before and considered joining for the commemorative launch, imagining a handful of pastel-colored balloons peacefully ascending into a blue, sunny sky. Instead, it rained, and the launch was postponed.

It never occurred to me that these balloon launches might be considered acts of war. Later I learned that local residents had voiced their concerns, claiming recent confrontations between balloon launchers and Sunshine Policy supporters had affected their businesses, tourism to the area, and sense of safety. In April of this year, North Korea even threatened to "mercilessly" shell the border towns if the balloon launchings continued.

I felt ashamed by how close I had come to blindly inserting myself in an activity with the potential to endanger the lives of people near the border. It was just proof of how much I had to learn about my new surroundings, and the inherent limits of my knowledge as a newly arrived foreigner. After all, since I wasn't fluent enough to understand all of Korean media, most of my news came from the English-language daily. Conversing with Korean activists in their native tongue still felt stiff, my words carefully constructed and calculated; interacting with other English-speaking foreigners put me more at ease.

But more than simply language itself, my lack of understanding seemed to root from a significant cultural gap. Although I'd been fed the American narrative of the Korean War, I hadn't grown up in a society that directly pitted North Korea as the "hostile enemy," a phrase repeatedly used by the South Korean DMZ tour guide. The tour was effective at making threats from an oft-ridiculed, hermetic country like North Korea seem real.

Trudging through "The 3rd Tunnel"—the largest of five known infiltration tunnels dug by the North Koreans to invade the South, I was nervous. According to my brochure, the 1,635 meter cavernous space is large enough in scale for "an army of 30,000 fully armed North Korean soldiers" to pass through within one hour. Navigating the dimly lit, cavernous space, my body tensed at even the water droplets that hit my hardhat and slid onto my back.

I could see everything as simplistic. I had no idea what re-unification might entail, nor would my life be affected if the South Korean economy couldn't absorb its cost, estimated from a few hundred billion to up to several trillion dollars. My perspective as an outsider, of course, allowed me the van-tage point from which to chastise South Koreans for being too "complacent."

As a privileged traveler who'd come to this country on my own terms, I was afforded the time and means to create an ar-tificial, leisurely life of sorts—one atypical of that of the aver-age South Korean. And though I hated to admit it, being Ko-rean American didn't make me any less of a tourist. I was someone who had paid to visit the border, free to peruse a number of gift shops full of toenail clippers imprinted with "DMZ" and "limited edition" plaques framing knots of "genu-ine" barbed wire fence, slapped with serial numbers.

War as Spectacle

Yet I was mad for all kinds of reasons.

I was infuriated by how the tour seems to reduce the war to a spectacle. I felt like I was on a bizarre wildlife expedition when the guide pointed out rare species of floral fauna in our jeep and led us through an exhibit devoted to the DMZ as a nature preserve. I felt ridiculous taking a group picture in front of giant, purple-colored block letters spelling "DMZ." I was perplexed watching a video narrated by a jolly voice claim-ing reunification to happen "someday," but until then, "The DMZ is forever." I rolled my eyes overhearing two non-Korean American passengers on the bus refer to the trip as another stop on their "Asia tour." I was irritated by the corny jokes cracked by the Latino U.S. officer, who swaggered around as our camouflaged tour guide.

I felt they were interfering with a journey that for me, felt personal. I assumed they couldn't possibly understand all of the pain associated with the war. But perhaps what I was more frustrated by were the limits to which I could understand it as well. I wondered what right I had to feel upset about a trauma from which I was spared.

Bruce Cumings, a leading expert on North Korean and East Asian affairs, offers a leftist, revisionist history of the Korean War, describing it as a civil war with complicated historical roots that the U.S. had little business in interfering.

He compares the U.S. bombing of North Korea to genocide, revealing that the U.S. dropped thousands of tons of napalm and 635,000 tons of bombs in Korea, compared to the 503,000 tons of bombs dropped in the entire Pacific during World War II. U.S.-related crimes were concealed for decades, including the massacre of hundreds of South Korean civilians and the more than 200 incidents of U.S. soldiers attacking refugees in 1950 and 1951; it was also extremely common for soldiers to rape Korean women. In one atrocity, the South Korean police executed 7,000 political prisoners while the Pentagon blamed the event on the Communists.

Other activists who have echoed Cumings' sentiment about the U.S. owning up to its sense of responsibility are often attacked as being North Korean sympathizers. U.S. and South Korean understanding of North Korean human rights is problematic, they say, because it ignores the fundamental causes of the problem.

The embargo and sanctions by the U.S. and its trading partners, for example, helped halt North Korea's development and contributed to its poor infrastructure and famine today. Denying North Korea's right to food and health over regime change is a form of crime against humanity, they claim. Improving human rights in North Korea requires engaging and de-stigmatizing North Korea, while increasing military presence makes it difficult to forge a diplomatic relationship with North Korea and approach issues like denuclearization and human rights. Some groups opposed the U.S. passage of the NKHRA, which was signed by George W. Bush and backed by right-wing Christian groups and pro-war think tanks, along with human rights organizations. By politicizing humanitarian aid and increasing sanctions against North Korea, they say, the bill has actually exacerbated the human rights crisis.

"Postmemory Han"

Though I considered myself a progressive, I had never considered this more contextualized view of human rights in North Korea, and I was confused about what to feel. Seeing so many Korean uniformed soldiers with sewn U.S. flag patches at the DMZ was startling, a visual marker of U.S. militarism and intervention. While talking to my father, I rattled on about U.S. self-interest, broaching the possibility that the war was a civil one between Koreans.

"Bullsh--," my father said. "South Korea didn't have the intent to invade North Korea. Kim Il-sung wanted a war, and he was backed by Russian ambition and desire—but it wasn't the people of North Korea who wanted a war."

"The U.S. certainly has some role in the division," he continued. "No country is all good or all bad—it has its own motivations. Korea was a victim between two ideological forces: communism and democracy. But there's no doubt that South Korea is indebted to the U.S. When the war broke out North Korea was already well equipped and supported by the Russians—they had strong intentions to invade South Korea and try to unite by force. Without help from the U.S. and the U.N., South Korea would have been demolished and become a Communist country. You and me, we'd be in the condition of North Korean people."

Shortly after my visit to the DMZ, I learned of a concept called "han." "Han" is a Korean word without an equivalent in English, but refers to sorrow and anger resulting from centuries of oppression, invasion, colonization, war, and national division.

Some academic scholars have referred to a specifically Korean American type of "postmemory" as "postmemory han." It is a feeling that has been described as "bittersweet longing," "unexpressed anger built up inside," "complex," "dynamic."

Yet I wasn't sure if I could claim "postmemory han" to be what I felt. Standing in cue on our last leg of the tour, we forked over 500 won (approximately 50 cents) at the Dorasan Station terminal for the Reunification Train, developed in 2007 to run across the DMZ. Although regular service has not begun, the train occasionally took workers and materials to Kaesong industrial park, an inter-Korean economic development [initiative] built in 2005 involving 120 South Korean companies that employ over 47,000 North Korean workers to manufacture products. Kaesong is located in the southernmost region of North Korea, just 16 miles away from Dorasan Station.

The man behind the counter stamped my commemorative ticket, pressing with care to make sure the ink doesn't smear. In reality, the ticket would take me nowhere. Passing through the turnstile, I crossed through the entryway outside into the bright sun. I expected it to be eerie, but everything about it looked mundane—the tracks, the rails, even the sign that says "205 km to Pyongyang."

Standing on the platform, I squinted into the distance. I could hardly see anything.

*"No attempt is made to see both sides of
the Korean conflict."*

Portraying North Korea as the Villain on Human Rights Is Unhelpful

Paul Watson

Paul Watson is a journalist. In the following viewpoint, he argues that Western journalists overemphasize North Korean human rights atrocities and de-emphasize South Korea's. He argues, for example, that North Korean acts of provocation are exaggerated and taken out of context, while South Korea's authoritarian National Security Law is ignored. He says that the Korean conflict is complicated, and he concludes that blaming the North for all wrongdoing is biased and unhelpful.

As you read, consider the following questions:

1. Who is Ro Su-hui, and why was he in North Korea, according to Watson?

2. What explanation does Watson give for North Korea's shelling of Yeonpyeong Island?

3. What explanation does Watson give for the sinking of the *Cheonan*?

Earlier this month [in July 2012] a shocking scene played out at Panmunjom in the demilitarised zone between North and South Korea.

Warm North, Cold South

Ro Su-hui, the South Korean vice-chairman of the [Democratic Front for the] Reunification of the Fatherland, was returning from North Korea where he had paid his respects at ceremonies to mark the 100th day since the death of leader Kim Jong-il. Before re-crossing the border to the South, he declared "Hurrah for the unification of the two Koreas!" to a cheering crowd and was presented with flowers by his hosts.

But as the grinning 69-year-old crossed the border, he received very different treatment by the South Korean border security. The watching North Koreans howled in horror as Ro Su-hui was thrown to the ground and carried off in a headlock.

The arrest made a very small splash in the Western media, which comes as little surprise because a story with a warm North and a cold South doesn't square easily with the message that has been delivered by media outlets in Europe and the US for the last two decades.

Reunification and conciliation are usually portrayed as South Korean concepts, while North Korea is seen as a closed state, hostile to such talk on "idealistic grounds"—a view perpetuated by media outlets' lack of interest in all recent North Korean initiatives. In fact it is almost impossible to find any piece of positive European journalism relating to the Democratic People's Republic of Korea (DPRK) [North Korea]. The days of Cold War pantomime journalism and great ideological battles might be over, but North Korea remains an area in which journalists have free licence for sensationalism and partiality.

Lesser of Two Evils

The lack of Western sources in North Korea has allowed the media to conjure up fantastic stories that enthrall readers but aren't grounded in hard fact. No attempt is made to see both sides of the Korean conflict: It is much easier and more palatable to a Western audience to pigeonhole the DPRK as a dangerous maverick state ruled by a capricious dictator and South Korea as its long-suffering, patient neighbour.

These roles are dusted off whenever there are flare-ups, such as the Yeonpyeong Island incident of 2010 when North Korea was condemned for firing shots at South Korean military and civilians in an "unprovoked attack". It was not widely reported that South Korea had been test firing artillery in a patch of ocean that North Korea claims ownership of or that North Korea's repeated demands for an explanation were ignored. While military intervention may not have been wise, it was far from the random act of hostility it was made out to be.

When the South Korean navy ship, the *Cheonan*, sank on March 26, 2010, the South Koreans accused their neighbours of having fired a torpedo. A detailed rebuttal by North Korea's military was disregarded by the wider world, as was the offer to aid an open investigation.

One of the South Korean investigators, Shin Sang-cheol, sacrificed his career to express his belief that the *Cheonan* had run aground in a tragic accident and with reports of evidence tampering circulating, even the South Korean public wasn't widely convinced of North Korean involvement: a survey conducted in Seoul found less than 33% blamed the DPRK. Nonetheless North Korean guilt was stated as fact in the British press.

Since the bloody coup of 1979, South Korea seems to have had journalistic carte blanche as the "lesser of two evils". While North Korean actions are condemned and derided, very few column inches are devoted to scrutiny of South Korea's president Lee Myung-bak and his oppressive policies.

The National Security [Law], of which Ro So-hui fell foul, gives the South Korean government the right to prosecute anyone speaking in favour of North Korea or communism in general. There are frequent reports of detention without trial, human rights abuses and clampdowns on freedom of speech. Both Koreas are quite justifiably scared of the other but when South Korea flexes its military muscles, the North is expected to watch passively with any attempt to do the same reported as an act of despicable brinkmanship.

Whatever your view on the actions of North and South Korea's governments, the hypocrisy of using one-sided journalism to label North Korea a rogue, propaganda-led state is surely self-evident and fans the fire of intolerance and animosity. The Korean divide is a complex, multifaceted political situation. Nobody benefits from turning it into a moral melodrama, and we should demand more from our supposedly impartial media.

"Food aid via the regime will not ben-efit those who are in desperate need, but [will] reinforce a genocidal system that leverages access to food as an un-ethical means of controlling the popu-lation."

North Korea Orchestrates Famine as a Tool of Repression

Robert Park

Robert Park is a minister, a human rights activist, and a found-ing member of the Worldwide Coalition to Stop Genocide in North Korea. In the following viewpoint, he says that North Ko-rea is not a poor country. Rather, he says, its people are starving because the government deliberately uses starvation as an instru-ment of repression. Park also states that North Korea systemati-cally tortures and oppresses its people. He argues that the inter-national community and South Korea have a responsibility to force the North Korean government to cease its human rights abuses.

As you read, consider the following questions:

1. Why did Vitit Muntarbhorn report that North Korea's famine was not linked to poverty?

2. Beyond the prison camps, in what ways does Park say that North Korea has been violating the UN genocide convention?

3. How does China aid North Korea in human rights violations, according to Park?

The Democratic People's Republic of Korea (DPRK or North Korea) continues to commit acts of genocide and crimes against humanity that are unparalleled in the world today in terms of brutality and loss of life.

Korean Famine

To date, over four million have died of starvation in North Korea since 1995. Photographs from Reuters' AlertNet published in October [2011] confirm refugee testimonials of a continued famine. The United Nations [UN] reports that over six million North Koreans, particularly children and pregnant and breast-feeding women, are currently at risk of death due to starvation.

Interestingly, however, studies indicate that North Korean refugees almost universally oppose government-enforced food aid to North Korea. Despite having family and friends currently at risk, they adamantly warn that food aid via the regime will not benefit those who are in desperate need, but [will] reinforce a genocidal system that leverages access to food as an unethical means of controlling the population.

The Committee for Democratization of North Korea, a coalition movement spearheaded by North Korean refugees and formerly led by North Korea's highest-ranking defector, the late Hwang Jang-yop, has frequently and emphatically condemned unconditional aid to North Korea as a form of appeasement, warning that aid has not reached the average dying North Korean but has been stealthily exploited by the North Korean authorities.

[*Witness to Transformation:*] *Refugee Insights into North Korea*, a study published this year based on interviews with over 1,600 North Korean refugees in China and South Korea by Stephan Haggard and Marcus Noland, found that a substantial number of refugees had no knowledge of the over a decade of international humanitarian aid to North Korea, though it at one point purportedly fed more than a third of the North Korean population. Among those who were aware of international aid, the vast majority indicated they were never beneficiaries and that food aid was instead diverted to the military and to the party elite.

Citing poverty or natural disasters as the culprit of North Korea's perpetual famine is misguided. Former special rapporteur on human rights in North Korea Vitit Muntarbhorn stated categorically in his final report to the General Assembly in 2010 that the DPRK, which has the largest per capita army and the highest military GDP [gross domestic product] expenditures in the world, was by no means poor. Mr. Muntarbhorn noted that North Korea has very large mineral resources and generates billions in export and trade, but that the profits from this activity are being used completely on the party elite and for nuclear technology development. He concluded and has since reiterated in interviews that the North Korean regime has the means at its disposal to feed its people and that the real issue is not a lack of resources but a military-first policy and misappropriation of funds by DPRK authorities.

In the 1990s, the DPRK was the recipient of more aid than any other nation in the world. Yet there is now overwhelming, verifiable evidence of the DPRK's systematic diversion of billions in humanitarian aid during this period, which is internationally recognized as one of the most devastating famines of the 20th century, with as many as 3.5 million North Koreans dying of starvation. At the height of the famine, the DPRK regime suspended commercial imports, diverting the money saved to strengthen its military and to continue its nuclear enrichment program. The regime spent massive amounts of money on military purchases, including eight military helicopters and 40 MiG-21 fighters. This methodical diversion of humanitarian aid has been coupled with a harsh penal system centered on executions and detainment in prison camps.

Auschwitz Now

Political prison camps provide a clear example of the DPRK's use of food as leverage in preserving its repressive policies. Following the Soviet example, political prisoners have been systematically starved since the regime's inception in 1945. Moreover, according to current special rapporteur on human rights in North Korea Marzuki Darusman, as many as 250,000 political prisoners, one-third of whom are children, are at present being forced to perform slave labor on starvation rations and are subject to brutal beatings, systematic rape and torture, and execution at the whim of prison guards.

For several years, outside observers and humanitarian activists such as former U.S. senator Sam Brownback have stated that the camps represent the worst abuse of human rights in the world. Yet, satellite images released by Amnesty International and Google Earth confirm that these camps continue to grow and hundreds of thousands of innocent men, women, and children continue to suffer inconceivable inhumanity and die in silence.

As with the Nazi concentration camps, the full extent of the regime's barbarism cannot be known until after liberation. Some of the most substantial and horrifying accounts of the North Korean prison camp system have come from former camp guards Ahn Myong-chol and Kwon Hyok, who, at the risk of being stigmatized or even punished in the democratic societies to which they eventually fled, have confessed to the atrocities and murders they personally carried out or oversaw in these camps. These confessions have included detailed accounts that suggest chemical and biological weapon experimentation on political prisoners is taking place systematically in North Korea.

Im Chun-yong, a former military captain in North Korea, spoke to [Arabic-language news network] Al Jazeera in 2009 about North Korea's lethal biological and chemical weapon experiments on physically or mentally disabled North Korean children. Ri Kwang-chol, a physician who defected from North Korea, confirmed this account, testifying in March of 2006 that the DPRK murdered people with physical disabilities "almost as soon as they [were] born" and that the regime perceived the practice as a "way of purifying the masses." It is undeniable that North Korea's cruelty towards disabled individuals mirrors Nazi eugenics.

Furthering the Holocaust parallel, in the immediate aftermath of a BBC report in 2004, Yad Vashem of the Holocaust Martyrs' and Heroes' Remembrance Authority in Jerusalem made an urgent appeal to then UN secretary-general Kofi Annan to act upon reports of "political genocide" in North Korea, stating that "only six decades after the utilization of gas chambers to exterminate European Jewry, North Korea has apparently employed them against thousands of its own citizens."

More than a Human Rights Crisis

Beyond prison camp boundaries, the DPRK has been violating the UN genocide convention through systematic extermination on national, ethnic, and racial grounds, embodied in a decades-long policy of killing the half-Chinese babies of North Korean women who have been forcibly repatriated by China. Moreover, it has extended its genocide on religious grounds as well. Before the Soviet-led installation of the Kim Il-sung regime in 1945, North Korea was home to millions of religious

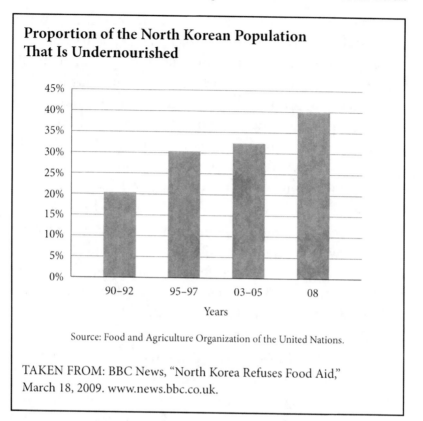

Proportion of the North Korean Population That Is Undernourished

Source: Food and Agriculture Organization of the United Nations.

TAKEN FROM: BBC News, "North Korea Refuses Food Aid," March 18, 2009. www.news.bbc.co.uk.

believers, including a burgeoning Christian population. Today, all traces of a religious culture have been obliterated. Recognizing the inherent threat posed by faith to totalitarian rule, the DPRK regime has, since its inception, sustained a campaign to suppress all forms of religious activity.

North Korea is consistently ranked among the world's worst violators of religious freedom. Open Doors USA, a Christian watchdog monitoring international religious persecution, has for the past ten years named North Korea the number one persecutor of religious believers. Open Doors USA believes that between 50,000 and 70,000 Christians are currently in North Korea's concentration camps. What is more, the children and grandchildren of any perceived political offenders are placed in camps as well toward North Korea's goal of fully eliminating the "seed of dissent."

Over the last decade, DPRK authorities have been able to dismiss recommendations from the General Assembly, the former Commission on Human Rights, the Human Rights Council, and the special rapporteur on human rights in North Korea. In response to a 2010 General Assembly resolution condemning "systematic, widespread, and grave violations of human rights," Pyongyang declared defiantly that it "would not change" and that it considered criticism of the DPRK's human rights crimes as a "political plot by hostile forces."

Indeed, the North Korean regime has proven itself most adept at employing deception in order to achieve its aims and stay in power. A prime example of such dishonest tactics is found in the pattern of belligerence and disingenuous engagement employed by the DPRK to win shocking concessions and consistently circumvent international efforts to curb nuclear proliferation activities.

In 1993, North Korea denied the request of the International Atomic Energy Agency (IAEA) to access its nuclear facilities after the agency concluded that North Korea had not honestly declared its plutonium production. While the [Bill] Clinton administration initially considered conducting air strikes to destroy North Korea's nuclear complex because of the compelling evidence that North Korea was preparing to build an atomic bomb, the United States instead decided to attempt to avert military conflict through negotiation. Former president [Jimmy] Carter went on an unauthorized visit to North Korea to speak with Kim Il-sung, and the two ostensibly reached a diplomatic resolution to the nuclear threat. The Clinton administration signed the agreed framework, which promised North Korea oil and other forms of developmental assistance in exchange for the dismantlement of nuclear plants producing weapons-grade plutonium.

Today, we know this deal to have been a complete failure. North Korea reneged on its agreements and secretly began enriching uranium immediately after signing the agreement, which provided an additional route to producing nuclear weaponry.

North Korean refugees and experts alike agree that the country will not voluntarily disarm under any circumstances while the current regime is in power, as the "military-first" dictatorship is profoundly dependent on its nuclear weapons program. The "cult of personality" at the heart of North Korea's political system would come under threat if the regime were ever to denuclearize, as doing so would doubtless be considered a national humiliation. Kim Jong-il and his cohorts take pride above all things in North Korea's military prowess. While they have diverted billions in humanitarian aid and resources to develop nuclear weapons and sacrificed millions of innocent lives, the chairman of the National Defense Commission is still praised by state media as the world's principal military genius. Moreover, as was evidenced by the DPRK's commentary on the Libya intervention this year [in which the United States intervened to help overthrow dictator Muammar Gaddafi], North Korea perceives the act of renouncing nuclear weapons as losing all leverage on the international stage. In a statement issued March of this year, North Korea accused the United States of disarming Libya through negotiations as a precursor to military action and asserts that the Libya intervention confirmed that the DPRK's military-first policy and nuclear arsenal were thus essential deterrents to invasion. It is clear that nuclear disarmament is not on the current regime's agenda, and therefore it is futile to continue attempts to bargain with North Korea about its development of nuclear weapons.

Necessary Next Steps

Through nuclear brinkmanship on the one hand and charm offensives on the other, the North Korean government has managed to deter a decisive and robust international response to its humanitarian emergency—a response that is exigent and long overdue. The testimonies of hundreds of thousands of North Korean refugees confirming that crimes against humanity and genocide continue in North Korea are overwhelming and unequivocal.

At the historic UN World Summit in 2005, heads of state and government leaders from around the world committed to protect populations from genocide, war crimes, ethnic cleansing, and crimes against humanity. Furthermore, they pledged to mobilize intervention when any given state manifestly failed to protect its populations or was the actual perpetrator of these crimes. Nations such as Guatemala and Rwanda, who had suffered genocides in the post-Holocaust era, stood at the forefront of this movement and demonstrated instrumental leadership at the summit.

Still, for the past two decades there has been no meaningful international response to the crimes against humanity continually perpetrated by the North Korean government. This international inaction is partially testament to North Korea's ability to blackmail and equivocate. However, another major obstacle has been China—North Korea's main accomplice. In contravention of its obligations under the 1951 UN refugee convention and its 1967 protocol, China has denied the office of the UN high commissioner for refugees access to the North Korean refugee population and continues to hunt down and summarily repatriate North Korean refugees in Chinese territory per a 1986 agreement with the DPRK. When forcibly returned, refugees suffer torture, imprisonment in camps, or execution, as North Korea criminalizes exit from the country. Hundreds of thousands of North Korean refugees, including tens of thousands of children, are estimated to be in hiding in China right now. The majority of these refugees are women, 80 percent of whom are victims of sex trafficking and abuse with no recourse to legal rights and protections.

Under responsibility to protect, the world has a duty to intervene first by "appropriate diplomatic, humanitarian, and other peaceful means" and then by force, if necessary. Due to North Korea's nuclear weapons program and China's role as its benefactor, protector, and ally, fulfilling this duty cannot begin without greater mobilization and louder outcries from the grassroots community around the world.

Additionally, there must be increased financial support for the surviving victims of the regime—the North Korean refugees. It has been confirmed through academic and government studies that thousands of refugees regularly send financial remittances to their family members or friends in North Korea via underground channels of either North Korean or Chinese activists. These remittances are important not only to meet the basic needs of the desperate population, but also to aid in exposing and undermining the DPRK system through empowering victims of the regime.

South Korea and the International Community

To address China's unique complicity in the refugee crisis, it is especially crucial for South Korea to take action. Though there are networks of South Korean and foreign NGOs [nongovernmental organizations] attempting to smuggle defectors from China to safer countries, they are able to reach relatively few of the refugees, an estimated one out of ten of whom is caught and repatriated to their peril during these "rescue" operations. However, the South Korean constitution extends citizenship to all North Koreans, giving this country the leverage to exercise its right of diplomatic protection over defectors in China. In the interest of maintaining friendly relations with the South, one of its main trading partners, China would likely feel pressure to accept the premise that the defectors have dual citizenship. Thus, South Korea stands in a pivotal position, as confirmed by the success of small-scale interventions by Seoul in recent months on behalf of North Korean refugees. The highest branches of South Korea's government must now begin to vouch more persistently and forcefully for the North Korean defectors on the grounds that these refugees are their nationals by law.

Still, the onus is on the international community at large to invoke its "responsibility to protect." General mobilization and mass demonstrations are key to revealing and responding to the mass human rights violations taking place in North Korea today. In what is one of the most devastating genocides of the twentieth and twenty-first centuries, strong, decisive, and swift international commitment to action must replace granting further time and concessions to the DPRK regime.

> *"The controversy over plying North Korea with aid has devolved into a struggle between conservatives and liberals."*

There Are Political Barriers to Providing Food Aid to North Korea

Donald Kirk

Donald Kirk is a journalist and the author of numerous books, including Korea Betrayed: Kim Dae Jung and Sunshine. *In the following viewpoint, he reports on political debates in South Korea and the United States over whether to provide food to help people starving in North Korea. Kirk says that food has become a political issue in the South, where liberals want to provide aid and conservatives feel such aid needs to be tied to political concessions on the part of the North. He says that there is concern that without monitoring, the North Korean regime will not distribute food to the needy but instead will keep it for elites.*

As you read, consider the following questions:

1. According to Kirk, what is Lee Myung-bak's view of North Korea's requests for food aid?

Donald Kirk, "Food Fight Looms over North Korean 'Famine,'" *Asia Times*, May 21, 2011. http://www.atimes.com/atimes/Korea/ME21Dg01.html. Copyright © 2011 by Asia Times Online. All rights reserved. Reproduced by permission.

2. What recent revelations does Kirk say complicate the effort to ship food to the North?

3. What does Peter Beck say would generate goodwill in North Korea?

The United States and South Korea are on a collision course over a pivotal issue: to feed starving North Koreans or not to feed them.

Talks and Food

The US envoy on North Korea, Stephen Bosworth, was in Seoul this week [in May 2011], carefully avoiding any commitment on the issue. He said in response to a question from this correspondent after meeting with South Korea's nuclear envoy, Wi Sun-lac, "We have a very strong common view of how to proceed on food."

Oh yes, he also said, at the same door-stepping interlude at the foreign ministry where he was besieged by a horde of writing journalists and cameramen, as far as the North Korean nuclear program goes, "the reality of coordination between the United States and South Korea is very very good".

The reality, however, is that the US is on the verge of deciding to send another US envoy, Robert King, on what's being called a "fact-finding mission" to determine how badly North Korea needs food.

King, the special envoy on human rights in North Korea, is not likely to pick up any "facts" the North Koreans don't want him to have, but the mission will likely be a breakthrough. It would, after all, open a dialogue between the US and North Korea that the North has wanted ever since Barack Obama's inauguration as president in January 2009.

Bosworth during his visit here is believed to have tried to talk South Korea's conservative leadership, notably Unification

Minister Hyun In-taek, into understanding if not acquiescing to the mission. He may even have told him that it will happen—regardless of his stance.

That's not good news for South Korea's President Lee Myung-bak. He has staked much of his prestige on a relatively hard-line stance that's reversed the "Sunshine" policy of reconciliation pursued for the previous decade by his two presidential predecessors, Kim Dae-jung and Roh Moo-hyun.

"MB [President Lee Myung-bak] can't be happy if the US does this," said Victor Cha, who served as Asia director on the National Security Council during the presidency of George W. Bush.

The whole thrust of Lee's policy, as enunciated to recent visitors, is that it is of paramount importance to hang tough in the face of North Korean pleas and pressure. Lee's view, as relayed by those who've seen him lately, is that North Korea is making a global bid for more food in order to stock up for grandiose celebrations next winter and spring of the 100th anniversary on April 15 of the birth of the late Great Leader Kim Il-sung, whose son, Kim Jong-il, took over after his death in July 1994.

Lee's position is that North Korea not only has to apologize for two dastardly acts committed last year [in 2010] in the Yellow Sea that took 50 lives—the sinking of the navy corvette the *Cheonan* in March in which 46 sailors were killed and the shelling of Yeonpyeong Island in November that killed two marines and two civilians. It was more than a year before the *Cheonan* episode, however, that Lee cut off aid to North Korea, demanding the North live up to earlier agreements reached in Six-Party Talks hosted by China to give up its nuclear weapons program.

Missiles vs. Nutrition

Now debate rages on whether the US should resume the Bush administration policy of giving food to North Korea, as did

South Korea during the decade of "Sunshine". Cha, a professor at Georgetown University and Korea chair of the Center for Strategic and International Studies, is not against sending food to North Korea if the US can extract an agreement "that would be as good as if not better" than the agreement reached in the last year of the Bush administration for "access and monitoring".

That's a qualification that many observers see as a deal breaker given the tight controls imposed by the North Koreans, but Cha thinks the Bush agreement had "to date the best terms". These were, "access to all provinces but two, [the] right to do nutritional surveys, permission for a portion of the monitoring team to be Korean-language speakers and one official on the ground," presumably from the State Department, "to monitor operations".

If the US can get all that, in Cha's view, "I think the administration would have a defensible position to give food."

The whole issue, however, is complicated by revelations in a leaked United Nations report that North Korea has been shipping missiles, and the technology to build them, to Iran via China, all in violation of sanctions imposed after the North's second nuclear test in May 2009 and the test firing of a long-range missile in April 2009. Those accusations, hotly denied by China and Iran, are certain to dominate attempts to bring about resumption of Six-Party Talks [with North Korea, South Korea, China, Japan, and the United States] on the North's nuke program as well as food aid.

Still, the whole question of whether to answer calls for help for people who are near starving after a harsh winter in which the crops were smaller than usual is a tough one. In a small gesture, South Korea's National Council of Churches this week shipped 172 tons of flour across the Yalu River border from the Chinese city of Dandong to Sinuiju on the North Korean side.

The Politics of Starvation

That aid won't go far toward relieving the agony of a country of more than 24 million people whose minimal need is estimated at 450,000 tons right now. Without the food, some analysts wonder if the North faces a famine similar to that in the mid-1990s in which as many as two million people are estimated to have died of starvation or disease.

Tim Peters, whose Helping Hands Korea assists North Korean refugees in escaping from China to South Korea, advocates more food aid via nongovernmental organizations (NGOs) but strongly opposes government aid in view of the North's current policies.

"I do think we should give it," he said, "but I'm very strongly against state-to-state transfers". He believes small NGOs "have their own pipelines". That doesn't mean they're not monitored, as is everyone who goes to North Korea, but essentially "they're off the radar of the big boys in Pyongyang".

As for massive state aid, however, Peters warned that "operating inside North Korea is a slippery slope" in which "you're used to using the regime". Foreigners, he said, "are so starry-eyed they don't realize they're being taken to the cleaners" adding, however, that a few NGOs over the years have "found ways to sidestep the main bureaucrats".

The controversy over plying North Korea with aid has devolved into a struggle between conservatives and liberals, many of whom were previously identified with the Sunshine Policy.

One proponent of aid, Moon Jung-in, a political science professor at Yonsei University, once close to Kim Dae-jung, said aid to the North was "long overdue".

He qualified that view by citing the need for "transparency" but believes the US State Department should have a good idea of where the aid is going—whether to those who need it most or to members of the armed forces, the government and the Workers' Party.

"They [the US] talk about human rights," he said. "Food is a very important part of human rights." King, if he goes to Pyongyang, "should use food aid as leverage".

Peter Beck, a scholar who has spent a number of years in South Korea, noted that sacks of rice with the symbol of clasped hands over the American flag, would "generate goodwill". At the same time, he said, "effective monitoring means no visits, no food".

As for the debate in South Korea over food aid, he said, "North Korea has not apologized" for the *Cheonan* or Yeonpyeong Island episodes. It denies anything to do with the former and accuses South Korean gunners of firing first in the Yeonpyeong clash.

"It's understandable there is reluctance," said Beck. "It's hard to feed someone who's literally biting the hands that feed you."

Periodical and Internet Sources Bibliography

The following articles have been selected to supplement the diverse views presented in this chapter.

Amnesty International	"Annual Report 2012: The State of the World's Human Rights: North Korea," 2012.
BBC News	"UN: North Korea Seeks Immediate Food Aid After Floods," August 2, 2012.
Economist	"North Korea's Prison Camps: The Gulag Behind the Goose-Steps," April 21, 2012.
Peter Foster	"North Korea Faces Famine: 'Tell the World We Are Starving,'" *Telegraph*, July 16, 2011.
John M. Glionna	"South Korea Security Law Is Used to Silence Dissent, Critics Say," *Los Angeles Times*, February 5, 2012.
Blaine Harden	"A Real-Life 'Hunger Games,'" *Los Angeles Times*, April 4, 2012.
Louisa Lim	"In South Korea, Old Law Leads to New Crackdown," NPR, December 1, 2011.
Matthew Pennington	"North Korea Prison Camps: 150,000 Languish in Secret Gulags, Human Rights Group Says," *Huffington Post*, April 10, 2012.
Josh Rogin	"So Much for U.S. Food Assistance to North Korea," *Foreign Policy*, March 28, 2012.
Choe Sang-Hun	"South Korea Arrests Activist After Unauthorized Trip to North," *New York Times*, July 5, 2012.
Kim Si-on	"Human Rights Violations in North Korea," *Korea Times*, August 29, 2012.

For Further Discussion

Chapter 1

1. Based on the viewpoints in this chapter, who do you think the Sunshine Policy would benefit more, North Koreans or South Koreans? Explain your answer.

2. Based on the viewpoints in this chapter, do you think that one's attitude toward reunification would affect one's attitude toward the issue of abductions? Why or why not? Explain your answer.

Chapter 2

1. Based on the viewpoint by Ralph A. Cossa and Brad Glosserman, is Chinese policy in North Korea logical or not? Explain your answer.

2. Based on the viewpoints by Doug Bandow and George Friedman, should the United States remove its troops from Korea? Explain your reasoning.

Chapter 3

1. Fred Kaplan argues that North Korea is not a direct threat to the United States. Kevin Rudd argues that it *is* a direct threat to Australia. Should the threat to Australia affect US policy? Explain your answer.

2. Evans J.R. Revere and John R. Bolton present differing viewpoints on how talks could affect North Korea's nuclear threat, while Philip Worré and Intaek Han argue that European Union participation in talks would reduce the North Korean nuclear threat. Who do you think makes the most convincing argument, and why? Explain your reasoning.

Chapter 4

1. Paul Watson argues that North Korea and South Korea both have human rights issues and that portraying North Korea as the villain is unhelpful. Based on the viewpoints in this chapter, do you think that it is true that North Korea is unhelpfully demonized? Explain your answer.

2. Based on the viewpoints by Donald Kirk and Robert Park, should the United States provide food aid to North Korea? Explain your answer.

Organizations to Contact

The editors have compiled the following list of organizations concerned with the issues debated in this book. The descriptions are derived from materials provided by the organizations. All have publications or information available for interested readers. The list was compiled on the date of publication of the present volume; the information provided here may change. Be aware that many organizations take several weeks or longer to respond to inquiries, so allow as much time as possible.

Brookings Institution
1775 Massachusetts Avenue NW, Washington, DC   20036
(202) 797-6000
website: www.brookings.org

Founded in 1927, the Brookings Institution conducts research and analyzes global events and their impact on the United States and US foreign policy. It publishes the quarterly *Brookings Review* as well as numerous books and research papers on foreign policy, many of which discuss Korea. Its website also includes articles and policy papers such as "Current Prospects for Change in North Korea" and "North Korea: Moving Towards Chaos or Reform?"

CATO Institute
1000 Massachusetts Avenue NW
Washington, DC   20001-5403
(202) 842-0200
website: www.cato.org

The Cato Institute is a nonpartisan libertarian public policy research foundation that promotes the principles of limited government, individual liberty, and peace. The institute regularly publishes policy analysis reports and op-eds that focus on foreign policy issues involving Korea, such as "A Free Trade Agreement with South Korea Would Promote Both Prosperity and Security." It also publishes books, including *The Korean Conundrum: America's Troubled Relations with North and South Korea.*

Council on Foreign Relations

The Harold Pratt House, 58 E. Sixty-Eighth Street
New York, NY   10065
(212) 434-9400 • fax: (212) 434-9800
e-mail: communications@cfr.org
website: www.cfr.org

The Council on Foreign Relations researches the international aspects of American economic and political policies. Its journal, *Foreign Affairs*, published five times a year, provides analysis on global situations including those pertaining to Korea. Its website includes numerous policy papers, such as "North Korea's Missiles, Nukes, and False Promises: How to Respond?" and "Inside Korea."

East-West Center

1601 East-West Road, Honolulu, HI   96848
(808) 944-7111 • fax: (808) 944-7376
website: www.eastwestcenter.org

The East-West Center was established by Congress in 1960 as an independent nonprofit organization. Its mission is to promote better relations and understanding among the people and nations of the United States, Asia, and the Pacific through cooperative study, research, and dialogue. It produces numerous publications, including the two-page *Asia Pacific Bulletin*, the AsiaPacific Issues series of papers, and the book series *Contemporary Issues in Asia and the Pacific.*

Heritage Foundation

214 Massachusetts Avenue NE, Washington, DC   20002-4999
(202) 546-4400 • fax: (202) 546-8328
e-mail: info@heritage.org
website: www.heritage.org

The Heritage Foundation is a conservative think tank that formulates and promotes public policies based on the principles of free enterprise, limited government, individual freedom, traditional American values, and a strong national defense. It publishes many position papers on US policy toward Korea, such as "North Korea Leadership Instability: Power Struggle in Pyongyang" and "North vs. South: How Economic Freedom Impacts Korea."

Human Rights Watch
350 Fifth Avenue, 34th Floor, New York, NY   10118-3299
(212) 290-4700
website: www.hrw.org

Human Rights Watch is dedicated to protecting the human rights of people around the world to prevent discrimination, uphold political freedom, protect people from inhumane conduct in wartime, and bring offenders to justice. Human Rights Watch investigates and exposes human rights violations and holds abusers accountable. Its website includes press releases, letters, and articles regarding human rights in North Korea and South Korea.

Institute for Policy Studies
1112 Sixteenth Street NW, Suite 600, Washington, DC   20036
(202) 234-9382
e-mail: info@ips-dc.org
website: www.ips-dc.org

The goal of the Institute for Policy Studies is to empower people to build healthy and democratic societies in communities, the United States, and around the world. It is the publisher of *Foreign Policy in Focus*, which offers articles such as "Environmentalists Stifled in Jeju" and "Korea and the U.S. Elections."

Korea Institute for National Unification (KINU)
123, 4.19ro (Suyudong), Gangbuk-gu, Seoul   142-728
  Korea

02-900-4300 • fax: 02-901-2549
website: www.kinu.or.kr/eng/

The Korea Institute for National Unification (KINU) is a hub for research on Korean reunification. It plays a leading role in laying the foundations for a peaceful settlement of the Korean division by advising policy makers, shaping a national consensus, and promoting peace and prosperity on the Korean Peninsula. It publishes the *International Journal of Korean Unification Studies*, yearly white papers on human rights in North Korea, and other reports, many of which are available on its website.

Nautilus Institute
2421 Fourth Street, Berkeley, CA   94710
(510) 423-0372
e-mail: nautilus@nautilus.org
website: www.nautilus.org

The Nautilus Institute is devoted to building peace, creating security, and restoring sustainability in the Asia Pacific region. In pursuit of this mission, it gathers together a community of scholars and practitioners to conduct research on strategies to solve interconnected global problems. Its publications include briefing books on topics such as North Korea and nuclear energy; reports, such as "Will East Asia Mega-Cities Be Secure and Sustainable by 2050?"; and numerous other articles available on its website.

United States Department of State
2201 C Street NW, Washington, DC   20520
(202) 647-4000
website: www.state.gov

The Department of State is a US federal agency that advises the president on issues of foreign policy. Its website includes a section titled "Countries & Regions" that provides a great deal of information about the countries of North Korea and South Korea, including fact sheets, news articles, and other publications.

Bibliography of Books

William E. Berry Jr. — *Global Security Watch: Korea: A Reference Handbook*. Westport, CT: Praegar, 2008.

Christoph Bluth — *Crisis on the Korean Peninsula*. Washington, DC: Potomac Books, 2011.

Gregg Brazinsky — *Nation Building in South Korea: Koreans, Americans, and the Making of a Democracy*. Chapel Hill: University of North Carolina Press, 2007.

Victor Cha — *The Impossible State: North Korea, Past and Future*. New York: Ecco, 2012.

Barbara Demick — *Nothing to Envy: Ordinary Lives in North Korea*. New York: Spiegel & Grau, 2010.

Jacques L. Fuqua Jr. — *Korean Unification: Inevitable Challenges*. Washington, DC: Potomac Books, 2011.

Stephan Haggard and Marcus Noland — *Witness to Transformation: Refugee Insights into North Korea*. Washington, DC: Peterson Institute for International Economics, 2011.

Blaine Harden — *Escape from Camp 14: One Man's Remarkable Odyssey from North Korea to Freedom in the West*. New York: Viking, 2012.

Uk Heo and Terence Roehrig · *South Korea Since 1980*. New York: Cambridge University Press, 2010.

Chua Beng Huat and Koichi Iwabuchi, eds. · *East Asian Pop Culture: Analysing the Korean Wave*. Hong Kong: Hong Kong University Press, 2008.

Kyung Moon Hwang · *A History of Korea: An Episodic Narrative*. New York: Palgrave Macmillan, 2010.

Son Key-young · *South Korean Engagement Policies and North Korea: Identities, Norms and the Sunshine Policy*. New York: Routledge, 2006.

Myung Oak Kim and Sam Jaffe · *The New Korea: An Inside Look at South Korea's Economic Rise*. New York: AMACOM, 2010.

Andrei Lankov · *North of the DMZ: Essays on Daily Life in North Korea*. Jefferson, NC: McFarland & Co., 2007.

Chae-Jin Lee · *A Troubled Peace: US Policy and the Two Koreas*. Baltimore, MD: Johns Hopkins University Press, 2006.

Jid Lee · *To Kill a Tiger: A Memoir of Korea*. New York: Overlook Press, 2010.

Chung-in Moon · *The Sunshine Policy: In Defense of Engagement as a Path to Peace in Korea*. Seoul, South Korea: Yonsei University Press, 2012.

B.R. Myers
The Cleanest Race: How North Koreans See Themselves—And Why It Matters. Brooklyn, NY: Melville House Publishing, 2011.

Mark James Russell
Pop Goes Korea: Behind the Revolution in Movies, Music, and Internet Culture. Berkeley, CA: Stone Bridge Press, 2008.

Michael J. Seth
A History of Korea: From Antiquity to the Present. Lanham, MD: Rowman & Littlefield, 2011.

Ruchir Sharma
Breakout Nations: In Pursuit of the Next Economic Miracles. New York: W.W. Norton & Co., 2012.

Scott Snyder
China's Rise and the Two Koreas: Politics, Economics, Security. Boulder, CO: Lynne Rienner Publishers, 2009.

C. Sarah Soh
The Comfort Women: Sexual Violence and Postcolonial Memory in Korea and Japan. Chicago, IL: University of Chicago Press, 2009.

Taku Tamaki
Deconstructing Japan's Image of South Korea: Identity in Foreign Policy. New York: Palgrave Macmillan, 2010.

Chris Tharp
Dispatches from the Peninsula: Six Years in South Korea. Hong Kong: Signal 8 Press, 2011.

Index

A

Abductee Support Directorate (South Korea), 59
Abduction of foreign nationals, by North Korea, 44–48
  denials by North Korea, 48
  firm vs. quiet diplomatic efforts, 50–52
  Japanese nationals, 44, 48, 52–53
  Kim Jong-il's admission of program, 44–48
  KNRC efforts at ending, 54–55
  NARKN interviews of agents, 46
  plan development by North Korea, 52–54
  South Korea's response, 49–61
  UN condemnation of, 45
  victim enticement strategy, 47
Ahn Myong Jin, 46
Airline hijacking, from South Korea, 45, 53
Amnesty International (NGO), 173
Auschwitz concentration camps, 173–174
Australia, North Korea as threat to, 107–111
Axis of evil rhetoric (of Bush, George W.), 39, 41, 42

B

Background Notes: South Korea (US Department of State), 80

Bandow, Doug, 77–81
Beck, Peter, 186
Biological Weapons Convention, 93–94
Biological weapons program (North Korea), 93
Boc, Anny, 72–76
Boh-ui-boo (North Korean intelligence agency), 158
Bolton, John, 129–133
Bosworth, Stephen W., 120–121
Bruce, Scott, 95–102
Bush, George W.
  axis of evil rhetoric, 39, 40–42
  failed negotiations with North Korea, 125
  mistake about North Korea, 117
  Sunshine Policy thwarted by, 22

C

Campbell, Kurt, 78
Carnegie Endowment for international Peace, 76
Carnegie-Tsinghua Center (China), 76
Carter, Jimmy, 96, 176
Cato Institute, 77
Center for Northeast Asian Policy Studies (Brookings Institution), 119
Center for Strategic and International Studies, 28

Central Foreign Affairs Office (China), 73–74

Central Military Commission (North Korea), 96–97

Central Party School (China), 73, 75

Cha, Victor, 183–184

Chemical weapons program (North Korea), 93, 94

Cheney, Dick, 117

Cheonan ship (South Korea), sinking of, by North Korea, 68, 79, 97–98, 106, 123, 168

China

  antagonism of neighbors by, 68–69

  battles with US in Korea, 41–42

  blocking of contingency planning, 70

  Central Foreign Affairs Office, 73–74

  Central Party School, 73, 75

  China's Study Times entreaty to, 73

  denuclearization vs. stability, 67

  enabling of North Korea's behavior, 67–68, 178

  Falun Gong spiritual movement, 137

  financial reforms in, 30

  illogical North Korea policy, 66–71

  Kim Jong-un's visit to, 97

  North Korean refugees in, 172

  North Korea's use to, 89

  Northeast Asia stability focus, 70–71

  opposition to North Korea's policies, 72–76

  potential political transition, 101

  reinforcement of US role in Asia, 70

  reunification resistance, 41

  security challenges, 31

  self-tarnishing of image by, 69–70

  Six-Party Talks participation, 29, 88

  strengthening of US alliance system, 69

  traditionalists vs. strategists, 75

  view of North Korea, 85

  violations of UN treaty obligations, 140

China-North Korea Relations (Nanto and Manyin), 74

China's Study Times journal, 73

Cho Gab Je, 46

Choe Sang-Hun, 14, 64

Choi Un-hee, 46

Chosun Ilbo (South Korean newspaper), 38, 58

Chung, Iris, 153–165

Clausewitz, Carl Philipp Gottfried von, 124

Clinton, Bill, 42, 117

Clinton, Hillary, 41, 122

Coercion, Control, Surveillance, and Punishment: An Examination of the North Korean Police State (Gause), 160

Cohen, Sacha Baron, 114

Cold War, 58, 83, 85–87, 108, 167

Committee for Democratization of North Korea, 171

Convention on the Prohibition of the Development, Production and Stockpiling of Bacteriological (Biological) and Toxin Weapons and on Their Destruction, 93–94

Cooper, Simon, 94

Cossa, Ralph A., 64–65, 66–71

Council on Foreign Relations (US), 64–65

Cumings, Bruce, 163

D

Dae Jung Kim (Gale Biography in Context), 24

Darusman, Marzuki, 173

Dear Leader of North Korea. *See* Kim Jong-il

Demilitarized Zone (DMZ)
  commercialization of, 162
  dangers in, 18
  ecological abundance in, 18
  Joint Security Area (JSA), 159
  map, 132
  North-South buffer zone status, 18–19
  Obama, Barack, visit to, 83
  signs of US intervention, 164
  small acts of war at, 159, 161
  tours and tour guides at, 161

Democratic Front for the Reunification of the Fatherland (South Korea), 167

Democratic United Party (DUP; South Korea), 22–23

Deng Xiaoping, 26

Deng Yuwen, 73

DMZ. *See* Demilitarized Zone

DMZ Forum (US), 19

DPRK (Democratic People's Republic of Korea). *See* North Korea

E

East-West Center, 95

The Echo from Darkness (Choi and Shin), 46

Economist article, 16

Engaging North Korea: The Clouded Legacy of South Korea's Sunshine Policy (Sung-Yoon Lee), 31

Epoch Times article, 140–141

European Union (EU)
  challenges in East Asia, 136
  humanitarian aid to DPRK, 135, 136–137
  North Korea denuclearization efforts, 135–136
  proposed Six-Party Talks participation, 134–137
  sanctions against North Korea, 68, 135

Expatriate (kyopo) activism against human rights abuses, 154, 156–159

F

Falun Gong spiritual movement, 137

Famine, North Korea's orchestration of, 170–180, 185–186

Fish, Isaac Stone, 15

Five-Plus One talks, 136

Food aid barriers, in North Korea, 181–186

Foreign Affairs journal, 27

Foreign nationals, North Korea abductions of, 43–48

France, negotiations with Iran, 136

Friedman, George, 82–90

The Future of War: Power, Technology and American World Dominance in the Twenty-First Century (Friedman), 82

G

Gause, Ken E., 160

Germany, 34, 36–37, 136

Global Times newspaper article, 75

Glosserman, Brad, 66–71

Guo Boxiong, 97

H

Haenle, Paul, 76

Hagel, Chuck, 73, 76

Haggard, Stephan, 172

Haidar, Mountaha, 46

Han (sorrow and anger), 164–165

Han, Intaek, 134–137

Han Sang-ryul, arrest of, 148, 149–150, 152

Han Sung-joo, 38

Harlan, Chico, 36, 142–147

Harvey, Fiona, 19

Hayes, Peter, 95–102

Healy, Hall, 19

Hecker, Siegfried, 126

Helping Hands Korea (NGO), 157, 185

Hemmings, John, 28–32

Hilton, Isabel, 39–42

Hippel, David von, 95–102

Holocaust Martyrs' and Heroes Remembrance Authority (Israel), 174

Hoon Jaung, 151

Human rights abuses (in North Korea)

atrocities against women, 158, 163, 173

defector testimonies, 144–146

expatriate (kyopo) activism against, 156–159

famine and starvation, 170–180

identification of assailants, 145–147

Kim Dae-jung/Roh Moo-hyun's concerns, 23, 31

need for accountability for crimes, 143–144

NGOs' action against, 157–159

strategy for dealing with, 25–26

Sunshine Policy and failure of, 31, 155–156

testimony about, 144–145

tortures in prison camps, 158, 173

See also Prison and labor camps

Human Rights Council, 176

Human rights violations, by South Korea, 148–152

Human Rights Watch, 148

Hwang Jang-yop, 32, 171–172

I

Infiltration tunnels (from North to South Korea), 161–162

International Atomic Energy Agency (IAEA), 116, 121, 176

International Covenant on Civil and Political Rights, 150–151

International Crisis Group, 76

International Security Information Services (ISIS), 134

Iran
  cooperation with North Korea, 130
  France, Germany, UK, negotiations with, 1136
  purchase of missiles by, 109

J

Japan
  DPRK's abductions from, 49–53, 57
  DPRK's nuclear threat, 41
  history with Korea, 64–65
  North Korea missile tests over, 125
  potential political transition, 101
  security strategy review, 76
  Six-Party Talks participation, 29, 88

Japan Policy Research Institute, 15

Jeju Peace Institute (JPI), 134

Jenkins, Charles Robert, 47–48

Jeong Gwang-il, 145

Jia Qingguo, 75

Joint Security Area (JSA), 159

Juche (Self-reliance) nationalist ideology, 32

Jung, Peter, 158

Justice for North Korea (JFNK), 154, 158

K

Kaplan, Fred, 112–118

Kim Dae Jung and Sunshine (Kirk), 181

Kim Dae-jung (S. Korean president)
  biographical background, 24
  human rights concerns of, 23
  Kim Jong-il's meeting with, 24
  Nobel Prize awarded to, 31
  repatriation of North Korean prisoners offer, 56
  Sunshine Policy instituted by, 21, 56–60, 154

Kim Gang-il, 145–147

Kim Guk Hwan, 140–141

Kim II Sung (North Korean founder), 38, 45, 96, 98, 176

Kim Jong-il (N. Korean ruler)

Kim Jong-il (North Korean ruler)
  admission of abduction program, 44–48
  failing health of, 40
  Kim Dae-jung's meeting with, 24
  nuclear weapons advantages for, 78–79
  pre-death power of clan promotion, 95, 97
  questions prompted by death of, 121–122
  reign of, 96
  sudden death of, 120
  unexpected shrewdness of, 117
  visit to China, 97

Kim Jong-un (Gale Biography in Context), 99

Kim Jong-un (North Korean leader)

background information, 96–98, 99
Chinese army delegation meeting, 97
leadership skills, 97
military superiority speech, 114
openness to new ideas, 34–35
rise to power, 29, 34, 40
role in decision-making process, 122–123
sea of fire threat to South Korea, 104–105
seeking of leadership continuity, 100–102
Supreme Leader status, 105
King, Robert, 121, 182
Kirk, Donald, 181–186
Kleine-Ahlbrandt, Stephanie, 76
Klug, Foster, 33–38
KNRC. *See* South Korean National Red Cross
Koh Yu-hwan, 105
Koizumi, Junichiro, 44
Koo, Jimmy H., 15
Korea Times article, 65
Korean Central News Agency, 104
Korean Central News Agency (KCNA), 104, 149
Korean Peninsula
Japan's history with, 64–65
Juche nationalist ideology, 32
Korean War destruction on, 18
missing soldier talks, 120
non-withdrawal of US troops from, 82–90
population density, 18
post-World War II division, 84
potential renewal of war, 72

reason for US troops remaining, 86–88
South Korean reconciliation efforts, 54–56
unification, problems caused by, 33–38
US commitment to maintaining stability, 105–106
See also Demilitarized Zone; Reunification of North and South Korea
Korean Peninsula Energy Development Organization (KEDO), 135–136
Korean People's Army, 96
Korean War, 14, 15
Cumings' leftist revisionist history of, 163
North Korea's memories of, 22
onset of, 84–85
post-war abduction program, 44–48
US role and strategy, 83–86
Korean Worker's Party, 79

L

Lee Hae-chan (DUP chairman), 23, 29
Lee Hong Koo, 19
Lee Myung-Bak, 16, 59–60, 131, 181, 183
Lee Yong-ken, 143
Lueth, Eric, 36–37

M

Mandela, Nelson, 24
Manyin, Mark E., 74
Mao Zedong, 30

McCurry, Justin, 103–106
Military superiority speech, by Kim Jong-un, 114
Miller, J. Berkshire, 93
Ministry of Foreign Affairs (South Korea), 134
Ministry of Unification (South Korea), 59, 159, 183
Missile test failures, by North Korea, 112, 113
Missile testing, by North Korea, 112, 113, 116, 126, 184
Mobrand, Erik, 49–61
Moon Chung-in, 20–27
Moon Yong Han, 140–141
Muntarbhorn, Vitit, 171, 172

N

Nanto, Dick K., 74
National Assembly (South Korea), 22
National Association for the Rescue of Japanese Kidnapped by North Korea (NARKN), 46
National Human Rights Commission of North Korea, 143–144
National Security Law (South Korea), 148–152, 169
Nautilus Institute for Security and Sustainability, 95
Negotiating on the Edge (Snyder), 115
Network for North Korean Democracy and Human Rights (NGO), 159
Neutral Nations Supervisory Commission (NNSC), 136
New York Times, 14, 75

Newsweek, 15
Nishioka, Tsutomu, 45–46
Noland, Marcus, 37, 172
Nongovernmental organizations (NGOs), 25, 151, 157–159, 179, 185
North Atlantic Treaty Organization (NATO), 137
North Korea
airline hijacking by, 45, 53
anti-American sentiment, 14
atrocities against women, 158, 163, 173
Australia threatened by, 107–111
biological weapons program, 93
Bolton, John R., stance against talks with, 129–133
bombing of Yeonpyeong Island, 68, 98, 106, 123–124, 130, 155–156, 168, 183, 186
challenges of negotiation with, 40
chemical weapons program, 93
China's illogical policy towards, 66–71
China's opposition to policies of, 72–76
Clinton, Bill, deal with, 42
Committee for Democratization, 171
economic collapse image of, 88–89
as exaggerated threat to the US, 112–118
famine orchestrated by, 170–180, 185–186
food aid barriers, 181–186
human rights record issues, 25–26, 140

invasion of South Korea, 14
isolation recommendation, 131–133
Korean Central News Agency, 104, 149
Korean War memories of, 22
leadership continuity, possible change, 100–102
leadership style shift, 98, 100
military prowess of, 177
missile test failures, 112, 113
money needs of, 48
nuclear testing program, 14, 29, 39–42, 73
Obama's statements about, 74
peace offensive resistance, 26
portrayal as human rights villain, 166–169
resistance to Sunshine Policy, 21
reunification, positives vs. negatives, 37
sinking of *Cheonan* ship by, 68, 79, 97–98, 106, 123, 168
South Korean POWs in, 53, 56, 58–59
South Korea's response to abductions, 49–61
spies and spy training, 43, 44, 48, 52
threat reduction by leadership transition, 95–102, 103–106
two-state federation vision of, 35
unstable war-like behavior, 109–111
US embargo and sanctions against, 163–164
US talks with, 120–121
weapons investments, 93
worship of money by, 23, 25

Yongbyon nuclear reactor, 42, 78, 96, 116, 121, 124–125, 127.130
See also Abduction of foreign nationals, by North Korea; Human rights abuses; Nuclear testing by North Korea; Prison and labor camps
North Korea Refuses Food Aid (BBC News), *175*
North Korean Defectors Speak Out (CBS News), 14
North Korean Freedom Coalition, 143
North Korean Human Rights Database Center, 157–158
North Korean intelligence agency (boh-ui-boo), 158
Nuclear Non-Proliferation Treaty (2003), 30, 109, 111
Nuclear testing by North Korea, 14, 29, 39–42, 73
  bomb-making capability, 107, 125–126
  Carter's negotiations efforts, 96
  China's support for, 81
  disarmament strategy, 115
  global fear created by, 88–89
  missile tests, 112, 113, 116, 125, 126, 184
  North Korea's nuclear history, 116
  Obama, Barack, push for renegotiation, 78
  plutonium supplies, 114, 127–128
  targeting of Australia, 108–109
  technical prowess limitations, 87

unwillingness to give up, 77, 78–80
uranium-enrichment program, 127–128, 177
weapon sales, 109

O

Obama, Barack
approach to talks, 122
demilitarized zone visit, 83
food aid link with arms accord, 113
meetings in Seoul, Beijing, Tokyo, 131
nuclear renegotiation push, 78
obligatory condemnation by, 115
post-election N. Korean nuclear tests, 130
statements regarding North Korea, 74
tactical errors with North Korea, 112
view of Kim Jong-il's death, 126
visits to South Korea, 16, 83
Open Doors USA, 175

P

Pacific Forum CSIS (Center for Strategic and International Studies), 66
Panetta, Leon, 122
Panjoy, Banjong, 47
Panjoy, Sukham, 47
Park, Robert, 170–180
Park Chung-hee (South Korean president), 52

Park Geun-hye (South Korean president), 27
People's Liberation Army (China), 75
Peters, Tim, 157, 185
Peterson Institute for International Economics, 37
Political prisoners and prisons, 31, 94, 143–144, 146, 163, 173–174
Popular Mechanics essay, 94
Postmemory han (sorrow and anger), 164–165
Powell, Colin, 117
Prison and labor camps (North Korea)
arrest of Rev. Han Sang-ryul, 148, 149–150, 152
arrest of Ro Su-hui, 167
Auschwitz concentration camp comparison, 173–174
genocide convention violations, 174–175
incarceration of Christians, 175
Kim Dae-jung's reluctance in addressing, 31
political prisoners, 31, 94, 143–144, 146, 163, 173–174
severe penalties and deaths, 158
South Korean prisoner reciprocity, 55–56
South Korea's exposure of abuses in, 142–147
tortures in, 158, 173
use of biological, chemical agents in, 94
Prisoners of war (POWs), in North Korea, 53, 56, 58–59
Pyongyang (capital of North Korea). *See* North Korea

Q

Qiu Yuanping, 73–74

R

Ramstad, Evan, 20
Republic of Korea (ROK). *See*
  South Korea
Reunification of North and South
  Korea
    Asian peace gains from, 133
    as Augustinian goal of both
      Koreas, 41
    benefits to S. Korea's
      economy, 34
    deterioration of cross-border
      ties, 106
    fixing of human rights abuses
      vs., 154–155
    German reunification com-
      parison, 34, 36–37
    inter-Korean summit (2000),
      154–155
    joint economic development
      initiative, 165
    nuclear program talks, 45
    peace dividend resulting from,
      37
    as possible détente moment,
      39–42
    potential costs, 35, 36
    potential renewal of war, 72
    problems caused by, 33–38
    projection of eventual
      achievement of, 71
    South Korea's support for, 35,
      36, 54–56
    vision of North vs. South, 33
Reunification Train (Dorasan Sta-
  tion terminal), 165
Revere, Evans J.R., 119–128

Ro Su-hui, 167
Roh Moo-hyun, 21–23, 29, 183
Rudd, Kevin, 107–111
Russia, 29, 88, 101

S

Sang Hun Kim, 157–158
Sasakawa Peace Foundation, 28
Scholte, Suzanne, 143
Sea of fire threat, by Kim Jong-un,
  104–105
Seok, Kay, 148–152
Shin Kwang Soo, 48
Shin Sang-cheol, 168
Shin Sang-ok, 46
Six-Party Talks
    Asian countries participation,
      29, 88, 101
    global ramifications of, 130–
      131
    issues of substance discus-
      sions, 121
    North Korea's withdrawal, 29,
      30
    proposed EU participation,
      134–137
    Russia's participation, 29, 88,
      101
    US participation, 29, 40, 88
Sneider, Daniel, 118
Snyder, Scott, 115, 117
Soon Ok Lee, 94
South Korea
    American troops in, 80
    anti-American sentiment, 14,
      90
    Cheonan ship sunk by North
      Korea, 68, 79, 97–98, 106,
      123, 168
    economics of reunification, 37

friendship efforts with North Korea, 179–180
hijacking of airline from, 45
Japan's military pact with, 64
military strength of, 169
Ministry of Foreign Affairs, 134
Ministry of Unification, 59, 159, 183
National Security Law violations, 148–152
North Korean prison camps exposure, 142–147
North Korean refugees in, 172
North Korea's abductions from, 43–48
North Korea's invasion of, 14
policy toward Falun Gong, 140–141
position on North Korea's human rights abuses, 153–165
potential political transition, 101
POWs in North Korea, 53, 56, 58–59
resistance to Sunshine Policy, 21, 28–32
response to abductions by DPRK, 49–61
reunification support by, 35, 36, 54–56
security strategy review, 76
Six-Party Talks participation, 29, 88
US security relationship, 80
South Korean National Red Cross (KNRC), 54–55, 59
South Korean Report Details Alleged Abuse at North Korea's Prison Camps (Harlan), 146
South Korea's Young People Are Wary of Reunification (Harlan), 36
State Council of the People's Republic (China), 76
Sung-Yoon Lee, 31
Sunshine Policy
   advice for S. Korea to not return, 28–32
   arguments in favor of, 29
   Bush, George W., thwarting of, 22
   chances for revival of, 26–27
   failures of, in N. Korea, 30
   false assumption of, 30–31
   influence on North Korea, 29–30
   institution of, 21
   origin of, 21, 56–60, 154–155
   realities ignored by, 32
   reassessment of, 20–27
   skirting of human rights talks, 31, 155–156
The Sunshine Policy: In Defense of Engagement as a Path to Peace in Korea (Moon Chung-in), 21
Supreme Court of Korea, 140–141
Syria, 109

T

Takayama, Hideko, 43–48
Thomas, Evan, 43–48
Traditionalists vs. strategists, in China, 75
Treaty on the Non-Proliferation of Nuclear Weapons (2003), 30, 109, 111
Tripwire: Korea and the US Foreign Policy in a Changed World (Bandow), 77

The Two Tales of the Korean Presidency: Imperial but Imperiled Presidency (Hoon Jaung), 151

U

The Uncomfortable SOFA (Koo), 15

United Kingdom (UK), negotiations with Iran, 136

United Nations (UN)
China's violations of treaty obligations, 140
criticism of North Korea, 45
missile launch denunciation, 113
missile test report, 184
North Korea's starvation report, 171, 172
nuclear-weapon free world goal, 111
political genocide report, 174
sanctions against North Korea, 76
2005 World Summit, 178

United Progressive Party (South Korea), 22

United States (US)
DMZ Forum, 19
embargo/sanctions vs. North Korea, 163–164
exaggeration of North Korea's threat, 112–118
food aid talks with North Korea, 182
killing of Korean schoolgirls, 15–16
Korean War role, 22, 83–86
Korea's anti-American sentiment, 14

non-withdrawal of troops from Korea, 82–90
North Korea as enemy of, 14, 15
political transition, 101
reinforced role in Northeast Asia, 70–71
secured release of Kim Dae-jung, 24
security strategy review, 76
signs of intervention at the DMZ, 164
Six-Party Talks participation, 29, 40, 88
South Korea security relationship, 80
strengthening of alliance system, 69
tactical weapons redeployment, 69
troop removal recommendation, 77–81

United States-North Korean talks
Bosworth, Stephen W., statement about, 120
Kim Jong-il's death and, 120–122
Kim Jong-un role in process, 122–123
reasons for re-engagement, 126–128
Six-Party Talks and, 121, 125
US position in talks, 122–126
Yongbyon nuclear reactor issue, 124–125

Universal Declaration of Human Rights, 150

Uranium-enrichment program, 127–128, 177

US Department of State, 80

US Treasury Department, 48

USA Today article, 15

V

Vashem, Yad, 174

W

Wall Street Journal article, 140
Walter H. Shorenstein Asia-Pacific
  Research Centers (Stanford
  University), 118
Washington Post, 36, 146
Watson, Paul, 166–169
Williams, Brad, 49–61
Woo-Cumings, Meredith, 15
Worldwide Coalition to Stop
  Genocide in North Korea, 170
Worré, Philip, 134–137

X

Xi Jinping, 76

Y

Yang Jie-chi, 76
Yeonpyeong Island (South Korea),
  North Korea's bombing of, 68,
  98, 106, 123–124, 130, 155–156,
  168, 183, 186
Yodok prison camp (North
  Korea), 143, 145
Yokota, Megumi, 44, 48
Yokota, Sakie, 44, 48
Yongbyon nuclear reactor (North
  Korea), 42, 78, 96, 116, 121, 124–
  125, 127.130
Yongbyon nuclear site (North
  Korea), 78

Z

Zainichi Koreans, 52
Zhang Liangui, 75

CPSIA information can be obtained
at www.ICGtesting.com
Printed in the USA
FFOW03n0941301013
2225FF

9 780737 769647